THE MANAGEMENT FUNCTION IN INTERNATIONAL BANKING

INTERNATIONAL BANKING SERIES

General editor: Steven I. Davis

Steven I. Davis:	*The Management Function in International Banking*
T. H. Donaldson:	*Lending in International Commercial Banking*
Nigel R. L. Hudson:	*Money and Exchange Dealing in International Banking*
S. M. Yassukovich:	*The Techniques of International Investment Banking*

THE MANAGEMENT FUNCTION IN INTERNATIONAL BANKING

Steven I. Davis

M

First published 1979 by
THE MACMILLAN PRESS LTD
London and Basingstoke
Associated companies in Delhi
Dublin Hong Kong Johannesburg Lagos
Melbourne New York Singapore Tokyo

Filmset in Great Britain by
Vantage Photosetting Co. Ltd,
Southampton and London
Printed in Great Britain
by W & J Mackay Limited, Chatham

British Library Cataloguing in Publication Data

Davis, Steven Ilsley
The management function in international banking
(International banking series)
1. Bank management
2. Banks and banking, International
I. Title II. Series
658'.91'33215 HG1615

ISBN 0–333–25930–0

This book is sold subject to the standard conditions of the Net Book Agreement

To Bob Stewart and Dewey Presley
for having given me the opportunity,
and to Joyce for having helped me
put it all in perspective

Contents

List of Tables and Figures

TABLE

FIGURE

Editor's and Author's Preface

In the summer of 1975, amidst the alarums and excursions of the aftermath of the 1974 international banking crisis of confidence, I made a first effort to fill a perceived gap in books written about international banking by practising—and hopefully knowledgeable—bankers. What emerged was *The Euro-Bank: Its Origins, Management and Outlook*—a volume dealing with purely international, or Euro-banks, operating in the London market.

Three years later, my brief is more ambitious—but, at the same time, more modest from a personal standpoint. The overseas activities of national banks throughout the world dwarf those of the Euro-banks and raise a variety of issues relating to the allocation of resources between domestic and international business. To deal with the immense breadth and specialised nature of these activities, I suggested, and Macmillan agreed, that the appropriate solution was to ask experienced professionals in individual aspects of international banking such as lending, money dealing and investment banking activities to write individual volumes on their sectors of interest which, taken together, would constitute a series of books providing a reasonably complete guide to actual international banking practice for the student, newcomer, or outside observer of the international banking scene.

In the three years which have passed since my first book was written, the trends visible then have been accentuated: even more intense competition with a depressing impact on gross margins, greater sophistication of corporate clients, the need to differentiate one's bank from an increasingly homogeneous pack of competitors and the growing importance of sovereign risk exposure. International banking has come a long way from its relatively passive, 'foreign department' status of the 1960s and earlier; it is truly big business for the major national banks in the world who have been obliged to move abroad to sustain earnings growth and protect their domestic clientele from the ravages of foreign competition. The senior international banker has been obliged by these external and internal challenges to become in many aspects more of a manager than a banker, a revolutionary development in a traditional industry where promotion has usually been a function of success in the business of lending money.

With the three above-mentioned specialist banking sectors well covered by Messrs Donaldson, Yassukovitch and Hudson, I have, therefore, appropriated for myself the topic of the management function in international banking—one which not only fascinates me personally, but which also represents the focal point of my own career in banking. My approach has been to provide in this volume an overall framework or 'umbrella' for the other books in the series, in which such central issues as the determination of objectives and organisational structures are analysed. While there is inevitably a bit of overlap—or even conflict!—with the other volumes, my intention has been to write this book from the perspective of the individual or individuals with overall responsibility for the international function. The book is what my good friend Professor Charles Williams of the Harvard Business School would call 'issue-oriented'; it tries to explain management behaviour within a framework of what can be regarded as the principal issues facing international bank managers. As a practising member of this fraternity, I have tried to maintain that delicate balance between understanding and objectivity. Whether successful or not in this endeavour, I hope that the book is useful to those for whom it is written: students of banking, newcomers to the trade of international banking, and outside observers such as central bankers, customers and academics who are trying to fit our behaviour into their own frame of reference.

My grateful thanks for their goodwill and material assistance in the preparation of this book go first to the 40 senior bankers who took the time to fill out and discuss a detailed questionnaire on how they run their international functions, as well as the 30 senior corporate officers who provided their frank views on the performance of international banks. I can only hope that they derive from this dialogue as recorded in the book a fraction of the usefulness it has been to me in broadening my own perspective and quantifying management and client behaviour and attitudes. My research labours were considerably assisted by friends at the Institute of Bankers Library, Salomon Brothers, the Federal Reserve Board staff, IBCA International Banking Analysis and Professor David Llewellyn of Loughborough University. Chris Batt of McKinsey and Company gave liberally of his time in providing the outside consultant's perspective. Tim Farmiloe of Macmillan once again played his usual co-operative and helpful role as my editor. And to Sally Watts, who has taken this tome from a scribbled draft to a final typescript with her usual enthusiasm and intelligence, I owe a special debt.

STEVEN I. DAVIS
London, September 1978

1 Introduction

This book is one of a series of volumes on the actual practice of international banking written by senior bankers with considerable experience in the specific sector which is the subject of their particular book. While market practitioners may not be the most articulate spokesmen of their trade, they hopefully bring to bear a unique insight which may not be provided by an outside expert.

Within this framework, *The Management Function in International Banking* has two specific objectives. First, it is intended to provide the contextual framework for the series by briefly describing today's international banking market and its antecedent institutions. Its second and more important objective is to examine the role played by the senior management of an international banking department or function and to determine how such issues as the setting of overall strategy, establishing an organisation structure and the management of an overseas network are resolved by different institutions. Other volumes in the Macmillan series will focus more specifically on such critical operational sectors as the lending function, money dealing and liability management, and the investment banking function. The viewpoint of this particular book will tend to be that of the head of the international department or possibly the chief executive of the bank, while the reference points of the other volumes will be those of his subordinates responsible for or actively carrying out the specific functions described.

It might be useful at the outset to define the parameters of our subject and explain some of the methodology used in this volume. By 'international banking' is meant the activities of a bank outside its traditional domestic market sphere which involve, to a significant extent, a risk, structure or transaction not encountered domestically—whether it be the traditional 'sovereign' risk such as foreign exchange availability and arbitrary acts of a foreign government, a network set up specifically for overseas business, or a foreign exchange dealing function.

Our focus is, therefore, on the uniquely international operations of domestic or national banks in countries throughout the world. A separate volume, *The Euro-Bank: its Origins, Management and Outlook*, deals specifically with international banks established and separately capitalised primarily to carry on an international Euro-currency market activity without the domestic market base of the banks discussed in this book.[1]

A second distinguishing feature is a concentration on banks whose principal activity is commercial banking—essentially the earning of interest differential income from the positive spread between loans and deposits. While this definition certainly embraces the so-called universal banks in Europe and elsewhere which have a significant capital market activity as well, it does not include institutions such as the US investment banks which are primarily engaged in the arrangement of finance and capital market operations.

In keeping with the behavioural, pragmatic approach of the series, the methodology used is an examination of actual management practices. Statistics will be used where appropriate to illustrate this practice rather than simply to describe market structures or current operating conditions. A substantial effort has been made to reflect international management practice of banks throughout the world. Several useful books have incorporated the views on key management topics of American bankers,[2] who not only represent the largest single segment of the international market, but also tend to be more forthcoming with views and statistics then their European or Asian counterparts.

INTERNATIONAL BANK AND CUSTOMER QUESTIONNAIRES

To provide such a broader and more balanced approach—as well as to compensate for the author's background and consequent limitations as a US banker!—the heads of international departments or their key associates in 40 national banks based in the US, Europe and Asia were interviewed in depth using a detailed questionnaire. In some instances it has been possible in the following text to quantify statistically the results of these interviews, but in most cases they have simply served to substantiate in a more general form the points made in individual chapters. The sample includes eighteen US, three Canadian, two British, thirteen Continental European and four Asian banks; these institutions are listed in Appendix A. A conscious effort was made to obtain a reasonably representative cross section of banks based on such factors as the relative importance of a given country in the Euro-markets—hence the high proportion of US banks—and regional as opposed to money centre institutions. While some banks with a relatively small international function were included, a deliberate effort was made to weight the sample in favour of the relatively experienced and internationally sophisticated banks who have confronted today's critical issues and can discuss their proposed solutions. The questionnaire itself is attached as Appendix B.

This sample of international banks and bankers does not purport—particularly in view of the reluctance of many senior bankers to discuss management issues with outsiders—to be a professional survey using appropriate sampling and other statistical techniques. It does, however, represent a serious effort to analyse management behaviour in a sector not particularly susceptible to easy quantification.

As part of the research for Chapter 6, a questionnaire was circulated to a large number of senior financial officers of multinational corporations and other major customers of the international banks in an effort to obtain an objective and at least partially quantifiable appraisal of the marketing efforts of these institutions. The 30 responses tabulated represent, in the author's view, a useful outside opinion on the strengths and weaknesses of such efforts—particularly in view of the relative lack of professional surveys on the subjcct which have been made public. Responses were received from a variety of large and medium-sized corporations located in the US, UK, Japan, Australia, Scandinavia and Continental Europe; the questionnaire itself is attached as Appendix C. Once again this is not designed as a scientifically determined sample, although some useful quantifiable results were obtained. Its principal purpose, however, was to bring out frank appraisals of bank performance in the solicitation and servicing of prime customers.

These two surveys are intended to fill—albeit in a very minor fashion—a portion of the statistical lacunae which today characterise the international banking market. Only in recent years have global statistics on the vital subject of sovereign risk exposure on the part of international banks been published by the Bank for International Settlements, while very few countries make available the extent and nature of their own banks' international loan exposure. While individual banks are understandably modest about publicising some of their less successful loans, there is less justification for the fact that only a handful of international banks—primarily the larger American institutions—provide the outside analyst with the key statistics necessary for an evaluation of the level of volume, risk and profitability of their international function. Within these constraints, however, every effort has been made to include in the text the relevant industry and individual banking statistics which have been made publicly available.

To place today's international bank manager in an appropriate historical context, Chapter 2 provides a brief synopsis of four types of predecessor institutions: the Renaissance family-owned international merchant bankers; the commercial branch banks which financed the international trade and development of the European colonies in the nineteenth century; the investment or development banks which channelled European capital exports to developing countries during the same period, and the American overseas networks established after World War I. This chapter utilises some of the admittedly fragmentary historical evidence of management behaviour to draw some tentative conclusions which might be relevant for today's international bankers.

Chapter 3 then sets the stage for the subsequent analytical chapters by characterising the Euro-currency market of the late 1970s which provides the current environment for international bank management. Without unnecessarily duplicating some of the excellent detailed volumes on the nature and structure of the market,[3] this chapter describes the challenges for today's international bank managers posed by the variety of changes in customer requirements, credit exposure, organisational complexity and other factors. Chapter 4 introduces a series of chapters on specific management subjects by a general discussion of the determination of objectives and strategy formulation, as well as the various strategic phases through which a typical bank may evolve as it moves from a passive service or 'foreign' department to a complex and aggressive multinational function. Included in this chapter are a discussion of the motives for developing an international activity, the key elements of possible strategies which can be adopted and the actual practice of bankers in terms of the priorities they establish and the extent to which objectives and strategies are articulated.

The following chapter focuses on structures and management processes established by different international banks to structure their organisation and decision-making procedure to achieve the desired objectives. The factors behind the choice of specific structures and processes and the problems encountered in implementing these are discussed along with issues such as relationships with the domestic operations of the bank, decentralisation of the decision-making process and the relative emphasis on individual responsibility. The subject matter of Chapter 6 is the marketing and business development function in international banking. Different strategies adopted by these banks at given phases in their evolution are outlined, and the various approaches to product development, pricing and actual selling of services and products are discussed. The responses of 30 multinational corporate borrowers to the questionnaire discussed above are incorporated in this chapter, and the criticisms expressed are related to banks' efforts to correct these problems. Emphasis is placed on efforts to develop market image and penetration through geographical and functional specialisation, the identification of target customers and the use of calling officers and the overseas network to market these services.

Chapter 7 deals with asset and liability management. Separate volumes in this series cover the lending and money dealing functions in considerably greater detail, but this chapter takes an overall view of the international balance sheet and discusses the specific issues of asset and liability management which are particularly relevant from the standpoint of the international department head. Actual and likely international loss experience, the credit decision-making process and some of the issues of managing world-wide dealing positions brought out by the interviews are discussed in some detail.

Chapter 8 discusses the management strategy behind the establishing of the various types of overseas networks and the issues associated with the management of these offices abroad. The key variables and criteria to be considered in opening up overseas are analysed, and a number of common problems of existing networks—duplication, poor cost-effectiveness, evolution of needs and personnel turnover—are covered. In Chapter 9 are discussed varying approaches to the actual measurement of international banking performance. The chapter covers the different profitability criteria used by bankers to judge performance and summarises the limited data on international profit performance made available by individual banks and gleaned from the author's in-depth interviews.

In conclusion, Chapter 10 summarises the principal problem areas likely to be faced over the next few years by international bankers. Possible management responses to these issues and other trends which might characterise the international banking market are also covered. Particular focus is placed on interview results and efforts by banks to deal with the intense level of competition prevalent at the time the interviews were granted.

2 Management Challenges and Responses: Some Patterns from Banking History

For the international bank executive embroiled in an agonising decision in the late 1970s, the experience of bankers several hundred years ago may appear a quaint irrelevance. But even a superficial glance backwards into the literature of banking history, despite its limitations for the banking analyst, can give the thoughtful modern banker some useful perspective on his own problems.

At the risk of over-simplification and reading too much into historical accounts rarely prepared by practicing bankers, one can distinguish several interesting phases of banking history which have some relevance for today's senior manager. While the magnitude and sophistication of the current international banking market force one to heavily qualify any historical parallels, it is difficult to conceive of any of today's management issues, structures or concepts which have not been confronted in one form or another over the last few hundred years of international banking practice. International banking institutions over the past five hundred years or so have been engaged either in the direct financing of international trade—essentially commercial banking—or the arrangement of loans to be placed with bank or non-bank investors—what is regarded today as investment or merchant banking. Some institutions have carried on both activities, while the original merchant bankers of the Renaissance era took speculative positions in individual commodities as well as arranged for their finance. In the following analysis of the available limited and fragmentary historical records, emphasis will be placed on the management issues faced by certain categories of institutions and how successfully individual managements dealt with these problems. With few exceptions, such as de Roover's excellent study of the Medici,[1] the banking historian has been more concerned with the elements of historical narratives—key personalities, significant dates, the impact of external events—as opposed to banking practice itself. As a result there is a relative absence of the microeconomic detail necessary to evaluate the risk and reward of the business actually carried on and the background to management decisions taken. By piecing together a variety of such narratives, however, it is possible to make some informed guesses as to the issues confronted by past international bankers and how they were resolved.

THE EARLY MERCHANT BANKING INSTITUTIONS

Four specific phases or patterns of international banking history have been selected for this analysis on the basis of the relative availability of information and their relevance to the modern banking environment. The first is the international merchant banking institution which flourished between the thirteenth and sixteenth centuries and is characterised by such family-owned and managed firms as the Riccardi of Lucca, the Medici and the Fugger. In addition to commercial activity involving the purchase and sale of commodities, these banks financed international trade among European countries and acted as bankers to the sovereigns of the day.

In the absence of a generally accepted international medium of exchange, foreign trade finance generally involved the lender assuming not only a credit but an exchange risk as well. Extending a loan to, say, an English exporter of wool payable in Venice in ducats at an agreed exchange rate, required lending the English sterling at an exchange rate with the ducat which was deemed sufficient to provide an adequate return both for the use of the funds and the assumption of the exchange risk. Ideally, this exchange exposure would be covered by a matching transaction—say the sale of the sterling bill to a Florentine importer—or lending ducats repayable in sterling to the same importer, but if the flow of trade between the countries was uneven it might have been impossible to arrange such cover.

Needless to say, if the bill proved uncollectable, or the correspondent bank making the collection failed, the bank lost its principal.

Lending to sovereign individuals such as the English and Spanish monarchs, the Popes, and various members of the European nobility involved a different level of risk. These loans were generally secured by physical assets such as jewels or a stream of future revenues such as customs duties, and were applied to a variety of budgetary purposes—usually to support a military effort. A hard pressed monarch would not only pledge current revenues but also hypothetical earnings stretching years into the future. The bankers often found it necessary to refinance themselves or lend new funds to maintain their status with a royal borrower and retain some hope of recovering on earlier loans. Given the voracious financial needs of princes such as Edward I of England and the Habsburg Emperor Charles V in comparison with the capital resources of their bankers, the latter soon found themselves lending a disproportionate percentage of their total portfolio as well as a multiple of their net worth to individual sovereign entities.

These family-controlled institutions with unlimited liability of the partners usually set up a network of branches in cities close to their borrowing and deposit clientele which reported to 'home office'—Lucca in the case of the Riccardi and Florence for the Medici Bank. Headquarters laid down lending and other guidelines, but the number of weeks required in this period to transmit such a message usually obliged the branch manager to take his own counsel when a rapid decision had to be made. The Medici Bank of Florence, for example, which was the largest banking house in the fifteenth century, insisted that headquarters hire all staff to ensure a high quality of personnel; letters of credit in favour of the clergy and nobility could only be issued on a cash collateralised basis, and credit limits vis-à-vis other banks and certain members of the Papal Curia were recommended to the various branches.[2] Successful managers were promoted to larger branches or home office, and each manager regularly visited Florence to review his branch's progress.

The final collapse of the Medici Bank came in 1494 after several decades of decline during which individual branches were liquidated as a result of credit losses, the confiscations and physical losses stemming from civil strife, and poor management. Losses exceeding branch capital were suffered from loans to such sovereigns as the Pope, the Duke of Milan, Charles of Burgundy and Edward IV of England, who renounced their obligations or were unable to meet them.

The Riccardi, a group of Italian families who operated a more centralised banking partnership than the Medici, were the principal bankers to Edward I of England in the latter portion of the thirteenth century. Funds generated in Italy were re-lent to Edward as part of such a close relationship that the Riccardi became in effect a branch of the English government.[3] A twenty-year relationship was broken by Edward in 1294 when, apparently due to losses elsewhere, the Riccardi were unable or unwilling to meet the King's financing requirements for a forthcoming war, and the family's assets in England were confiscated.

The Fugger Bank's principal activity during its period of prominence in the sixteenth century was the financing of the Habsburg Emperors Maximilian and Charles V.[4] Funding themselves in large part on a three to six month rollover basis in the Antwerp money market, they lent at a gross margin of roughly 4 per cent per annum to the Habsburgs on a collateralised basis: the pledge of jewellery and the revenues from mines, customs and crown lands. But recovery proved difficult in the 1550s as the Habsburgs became more deeply involved in the expensive business of defending their Empire, and when the Dutch government, which had guaranteed the Emperor's obligations, defaulted in 1557, the Fuggers fired the agent who had made the original loans. Over the following century, new loans and refinancings were succeeded by formal bankruptcies by the Spanish state with work-out solutions involving reduced interest and extended maturities which affected the bulk of the Fugger's loan fortfolio until 1650, when the bank was finally obliged to write off Habsburg obligations representing most of the bank's profits over the previous century.

From these tales of Renaissance merchant banking woe, the historians themselves have drawn their own conclusions. Referring to the downfall of Edward I's bankers, Richard Kaeuper points out that 'however seductive the profits and privileges awaiting the king's bankers, the relationship was inevitably fatal for them. In England the Frescobaldi, the Bardi and the Peruzzi learned this hard lesson in the course of the fourteenth century.'[5] Examining the manifold causes of the Medici collapse, de Roover focuses on the management factor: '... techniques have changed, but human problems have remained the same. How to pick out the right person and put him in the right place was as much a problem for the Medici as it is in business today.'[6] Mixing banking with politics also played a role: he refers to the 'congenital defect of ... the financial type of sedentary merchant to drift from private banking into government finance'.[7]

THE NINETEENTH-CENTURY COMMERCIAL BANKS

A second relevant stage in international banking took place during the ninteenth century when new expatriate-owned commercial banks with growing branch networks were established in developing colonial territories, principally in the British Empire, to finance the international commodity trade which was the basis of their host country's economic potential. The histories of institutions such as the Hong Kong and Shanghai Banking Corporation, the Standard Bank (now Standard and Chartered Bank) in Africa, Bank of London and South America (now part of the Lloyds Bank group) and National Bank of India (now part of Grindlays Bank Ltd), trace pioneering banking efforts in which foreign-owned and managed banks were able to survive and prosper in relatively primitive economies despite wild swings in commodity export prices, civil and military strife, sharp currency fluctuations and significant loan losses attributable to poor management judgement. In their fluid environment, some of these institutions, in the absence of an indigenous lender of last resort, often assumed such central banking attributes as that of note issue.

In most cases these institutions were managed in the field by relatively young expatriate bankers who, given a communications time lag even greater than was the case with the Medici bankers in Europe, sank or swam on their own merits. Home office—generally in London—laid down general policy guidelines: for example, B.O.L.S.A. branch managers were to assume no exchange exposure in their lending book; to finance only short-term, self-liquidating trade transactions; and never to lend to local governments or against mortgages and securities.[8] Such conservative lending principles, coupled with a high level of liquidity in the face of the perennial local bank crashes, civil strife and periodic government defaults, ensured that B.O.L.S.A. was one of a limited number of survivors of the nineteenth-century Latin American banking scene.

Another survivor in a different marketplace was the Hong Kong and Shanghai Banking Corporation, which was founded in 1865 as the first bank owned by Hong Kong businessmen and dedicated to the China Trade: the three-cornered exchange of opium, tea and silk using silver as the general medium of exchange. The new bank got off to a difficult start: the Overend Gurney collapse in London brought about the failure of six of the eleven foreign-owned banks functioning in Hong Kong within a year of the Hong Kong Bank's start-up.[9] Its first two Chief Managers were asked by the Board to leave as the result of significant early loan losses.

Despite assuming both a credit and exchange risk on its loans—silver was the principal lending currency, repayable in sterling at a fixed rate—the Hong Kong Bank successfully managed both its exchange and credit exposure despite a sharp decline in the value of silver against sterling in the 1870s. Profitable branches were opened throughout the Pacific Basin as the bank followed the China Trade pattern based on China's key imports and exports. The bank became involved in sovereign risk lending on a secured basis when the Manchu Dynasty began in 1863 to borrow against the security of customs receipts which by agreement were controlled by British government officials. A number of such loans were managed by the Hong Kong Bank and sold in London and Hong Kong; its success is perhaps best described by the comment of the British head of Chinese Customs on one particular loan: 'the Bank made hugely by it'.[10] While the Manchus collapsed and the new Republican government foundered in the period prior to World War I, the Bank continued to float successfully a variety of loans for railways and projects secured by the individual projects or specific revenue from customs or the salt monopoly.

The National Bank of India, which was engaged since its founding in 1863 in the financing of India's export and import trade, was also one of the few survivors of the crash of the 1860s associated with the Overend Gurney collapse and the opening up of the US cotton market. Branches were established in a variety of countries trading with India, despite early loan losses which resulted in the offending manager making personal restitution and another branch manager being obliged to put up a personal guaranty before assuming his new position.[11] Once again, credit as well as currency risks were taken as the bank's capital was denominated in sterling while its loans were primarily in rupees.

A final example of the nineteenth-century 'colonial' commercial bank is the Standard Bank which was set up in 1863 to finance the South African wool trade. Bad debts inevitably increased during the periodic collapses of wool prices, but exchange losses were minimised by a policy of matching currency exposures and reducing loans in Africa, rather than increasing the bank's sterling overdraft facility at home office in London.[12] Following the discovery of mineral wealth in South Africa, the bank emphasised loans against the minerals themselves rather than mortgages or equity shares; some losses, however, were still incurred when the latter declined.

THE NINETEENTH-CENTURY INVESTMENT AND UNIVERSAL BANKS

A third historical banking phenomenon was the several hundred universal banks established during the nineteenth century, one of whose principal activities was the channelling of European capital exports in the form of fixed rate, long-term loans to the developing countries of that period. In their role as promoters of railway and other projects they played the role of today's development or investment banks. Income took the form of underwriting and other fees earned on loan placements as well as interest income derived from the portion of these issues held in portfolio.

One sub-category of these universal banks was the large number of relatively new commercial banks such as the Mitsui Bank,[13] Deutsche Bank,[14] and Société Générale de Belgique,[15] established in the countries with more recent colonial interests, which also financed trade between the home country and its economic outposts abroad through a growing network of overseas branches and subsidiaries. By 1914, for example, the German overseas banks had 53 branches in Latin America alone.[16] Another sub-category was the family-owned and managed merchant banks such as Rothschilds, Barings, and Hope and Co. which had been established earlier but now achieved a level of prominence.

Perhaps the most interesting category, however, consisted of investment banks set up in the 1850s and 1860s specifically to arrange finance for capital importing countries such as Turkey, Sweden, Italy, Egypt, Spain, Russia and the Latin American republics. Often promoted by other banking institutions who sold stock to individual investors, these new ventures were supposed to introduce European capital and project expertise into countries which represented, according to the prospectuses, the wave of the future.

A typical structural pattern involved a branch or home office in London to tap the sterling interbank and capital markets, and business development offices in countries such as Turkey, Egypt, Latin America and the US. Among the survivors of this era were institutions such as Rothschilds and Barings with an effective overseas credit information network, usually in the form of family ties abroad. While Barings, for example, required Bank of England assistance in 1890 because of its holdings of unsaleable Latin American bonds and heavy commitments in Russia, its lending and placement record in the US was excellent, in large part due to its good sources of credit information and conservative lending policies by which the bank was 'not carried away by the excitement of the times'.[17]

In an atmosphere reminiscent of the competition in the late 1970s for mandates to raise syndicated bank loans for sovereign borrowers, these universal banks often appeared more concerned with the earning of arrangement fees than the creditworthiness of the borrower. Generous underwriting and placement fees—the Swedish Government paid Hope and Co. up to 9½ per cent flat for one loan[18]—were augmented by earnings from the deposited proceeds plus capital profits hopefully earned from selling the bonds at a higher price than the discount at which they were purchased from the borrower. In the view of one observer: 'any government which claimed sovereignty over a bit of the earth's surface and a fraction of its inhabitants could find a financial agent in London and a purchaser for his bonds'.[19]

Today's project financing experts would probably be appalled by the quality of feasibility studies for railways built in the four corners of the earth but which were nevertheless able to raise

100 per cent finance in fixed rate debt floated in Europe. European investors looking for higher yields than those available in London or Paris appeared undeterred by periodic waves of defaults which occurred when refinancings could not be arranged because of economic and political problems. In 1873 and 1874 alone, Turkey, Egypt and Spain, as well as half a dozen Latin American governments and roughly half of the US railway companies, defaulted on their foreign obligations. The impact of such defaults on the banks themselves varied substantially, not only as a function of the banks' discretion in choice of borrower but also, presumably, as a consequence of their relative skill and judgement in off-loading their commitments on outside investors. The record of the great majority of the newly-formed investment banks in the 1860s is particularly dismal, The Crédit Mobilier in France, perhaps the prototype of the new institutions, collapsed after an existence of fifteen years during which it launched a variety of subsidiary banks and railway projects throughout Europe.[20] Economic depression, mismanagement and an underestimation of the problems of launching a major project in developing countries all contributed to its demise. Overseas branches of the European universal banks, however, tended to fare better than subsidiaries or joint venture institutions which tended to be less closely controlled by the parent.[21]

One expert estimates that more than half of the several hundred new international banks set up in the boom period between 1856 and 1865 eventually proved abortive, while perhaps one-quarter of the total were insolvent within five years.[22] A sad litany of loan losses, defaults by sovereign entities, inadequate management and foreign exchange losses brought down such creations of the 1860s as the Union Bank of England and France, Continental Bank Corporation, the Anglo-Italian Bank and the Madrid Bank.

US BANKS AFTER WORLD WAR I

A final phase of international banking history of interest to today's manager is the expansion of US banks abroad in the period between World Wars I and II. Encouraged by the rise of the dollar as a leading international currency, the increase in US corporate investment abroad, and the passage of the Federal

Reserve Act in 1914 which facilitated overseas banking expansion, US banks set up networks of branches and subsidiaries abroad for the first time. Their principal objective was to finance US foreign trade and investment, particularly with the Latin American commodity producers, and for the first time dollar acceptances and letters of credit became widely used. From 26 foreign offices and branches at the end of 1916, US banks had 181 such operations abroad by the end of 1920.[23] Of the latter, 81 belonged to five foreign banking corporations, which foreshadowed today's consortium banks in their multiple ownership by US financial institutions.

The 1921 recession and sharp post-World War I drop in commodity prices, which had previously supported a large portion of the US banks' loans in areas such as Latin America, was certainly a factor in the credit losses and consolidation phase which took place subsequent to 1920. But other factors also lay behind the drop in US bank offices abroad from 181 in 1920 to 107 in 1926 and the liquidation or sale of all the consortium-owned foreign banking corporations. The familiar problems of inexperienced management, excessive expansion and competition for business are regularly cited in accounts of this period. As Phelps pointed out, 'the expansion was unduly rapid and unwarranted; trained men for the management of foreign branch banks were lacking. . . . They lowered rates, incurring the antagonism of native institutions, and granted credit upon anything but sound bases.'[24]

Chastened by the problems of lending to developing countries and volatile commodity prices (which collapsed again in the early 1930s and brought further losses to banks active in Latin America), US banks turned in the late 1920s to European countries such as Germany, which was then regarded as a first class credit. Acceptance credits were offered to German and Austrian banks until, in March 1931, Germany represented 40 per cent of all US short-term claims on foreigners.[25] Beset by the problems of the Depression and the 1931 banking crisis, the German banks could not roll over these credits and a standstill agreement, which froze the credits, was reached. The extent of the US banks' international commitment at the time was indicated by the estimate that 90 US banks were involved in these standstill arrangements.[26] In the decade prior to World War II, a classic work-out took place with periodic partial repayments, conversion into local currency which could be sold at a discount or converted into real assets, and write-offs of the balance.

With the benefit of perfect hindsight into this debacle, one observer blamed competition: 'each lending country operated on its own without apparent regard for the loans and credits showered upon the central European borrowers by their rivals in other countries'.[27] One defender of the banks in a US Senate investigation offered some of the time-honoured justifications of banking behaviour: 'we were perfectly justified in following the example of . . . England . . . and . . . Holland, who in proportion to their resources, gave larger short term credits to Germany than America did. . . . It may be locked up for a while, but that is the ordinary risk of business.'[28]

Perhaps the overwhelming impression from this admittedly fragmentary and often superficial view of historical patterns is that very few, if any, of the key issues faced today by international bankers have never graced a Board agenda before. Inexperienced and fraudulent management, the influence of greed in credit decision-making, the problems of lending to sovereign borrowers, over-concentration of lending, inadequate control and guidelines from home office, foreign exchange losses stemming from an inability or unwillingness to obtain cover, and the vulnerability of any international banker to political and economic forces beyond his control—all these problems are as relevant today as they were hundreds of years ago. Today's environment, which involves the support and regulatory controls of central banking institutions, as well as better communications and management information, is undoubtedly different, but the key factors involved in management survival and success have not changed significantly over the centuries.

3 The Euro-currency Markets: A Unique Management Challenge

To fully grasp the context in which international bank management functions, it might be useful at this point to sketch out the broad parameters of the Euro-currency markets. This chapter will also describe the management challenges posed by such related developments as the increased sophistication and changing needs of corporate clients, the increased emphasis on sovereign risk and the variety of specialist functions with which a senior international banker must deal.

While other relatively unregulated international banking markets have existed in individual cities in the past, such as Antwerp in the sixteenth century and the sterling market in London in the period until World War I, the Euro-currency deposit and lending markets are absolutely unique historically in terms of physical size, number of participating banks, world-wide scope, and importance not only to bank profits throughout the world but also to the smooth functioning of the international monetary system.

ORIGINS AND DEVELOPMENT OF THE EURO-MARKETS

The core of the Euro-currency markets is a broadly-based and efficient interbank market dealing in offshore-owned deposits and foreign exchange which provide a significant portion of the lending base for the typical bank with an international activity. Based in London and using the US dollar as its principal currency, the market now functions in other centres, from Bahrain to Singapore, and includes most of the currencies employed in international finance. Closely tied to it is the syndicated loan market, where term loans at a floating rate of interest to government and corporate borrowers are syndicated by telex and telephone to the hundreds of banks around the world interested in adding to their portfolio of international assets. Around these have grown up primary and secondary markets in fixed and floating rate negotiable instruments such as Euro-bonds, bank certificates of deposit, and floating rate notes. While several of these markets are based on non-bank investors and participants, international banks are active in them as a manager as well as underwriter and participant.

The twin concepts of an unregulated interbank deposit market in an international financial centre and of international loan syndication among these banks are not new,[1] but what is historically unique is the extent to which the Euro-markets have become a critical structural element in the forward calculations of hundreds of banks throughout the world, most of which had no significant business outside their borders until the Euro-currency markets developed in the late 1960s and early 1970s. Behind the early development of the markets were the internationalisation and rapid growth of corporate business following World War II, the availability of vast amounts of US dollars supplied by the US current and capital account deficits of this period, and the various attempts by national authorities in the US, Germany and elsewhere to regulate monetary conditions in their national markets, which encouraged the flow of funds to and from the unregulated offshore Euro-currency markets.

More recently, added stimulus to growth has been provided by the role played by private financial institutions in channelling the massive international funds flows stemming from such recent developments as the increase in the world price of oil, the recession of 1974–5 and the rapid industrialisation of the developing world. With these financing requirements well established, an increasing number of banks throughout the world have become aware of the profit and growth potential of an international deposit and lending function. Whereas until the early 1970s most national banks regarded the Euro-currency markets principally as an opportunity to attract or lay off surplus funds in the context of their domestic business, the relative stagnation of domestic lending business in the major national economies since the 1974–5 recession has impelled an increasing number of banks with little previous natural business abroad to look to the international markets to sustain overall profit and asset growth. The relative ease of entry for a reputable national bank or its affiliates and the ability to add assets and liabilities without the long development period typical of national banking markets clearly facilitated such a decision. Banks which established overseas branches for domestic funding purposes in the late 1960s, therefore, found themselves actively engaged in lending these funds to foreign multinational and sovereign risk borrowers when the domestic requirement disappeared.

The impact of these successive stimuli is vividly demonstrated in Tables 3.1 and 3.2. Table 3.1 plots the physical growth since

TABLE 3.1 Growth of Gross Euro-currency Market, 1970–7 (amounts in $ billions)

As of end	As defined by Bank for International Settlements		As defined by Morgan Guaranty Trust Company	
	Amount	% Increase over prior year	Amount	% Increase over prior year
1970	78.3	—	110.0	—
1971	100.1	27.8	145.0	31.8
1972	131.8	31.7	200.0	37.9
1973	187.6	42.3	305.0	52.5
1974	215.1	14.7	370.0	21.3
1975	258.2	20.0	455.0	23.0
1976	305.3	18.2	560.0	23.1
1977	373.8	22.4	660.0	17.9

Source: David Llewellyn, *Trends in International Banking and Capital Markets.*

1970 of the gross Euro-currency market as defined by the Bank for International Settlements and Morgan Guaranty Trust Company. The former includes only foreign currency claims of banks in eight major European countries against non-residents, while the latter includes banks in a variety of other countries as well as foreign currency claims on residents. What is unique is not only the physical size of the market, which dwarfs most national money supply totals, but also its steady and consistent quarter-to-quarter expansion. In none of the seven years listed in the table did year-to-year growth drop below 15 per cent per annum; the latter rate was achieved in 1974, the year of the greatest crisis of confidence known in international banking following World War II. This growth has taken place despite repeated forecasts of a likely shrinking or actual collapse of the market as a result of factors such as the removal of US exchange controls and the crisis of banking confidence in 1974, related to the collapse of the Franklin National Bank and Bankhaus Herstatt.

Table 3.2 provides a rough breakdown of the overall Euro-currency market by categories of participant and geographic location between 1974 and 1977. The overall importance of American banks with their overseas branches, which represent over 50 per cent of the total market, is reflected in this data, as well as the importance of London, despite a steady decline in relative position, as the single largest Euro-currency market with 24 per cent of the total in 1977.

Of equal interest from a management standpoint is the extraordinary proliferation of new overseas implantations—representative offices, branches and subsidiaries—as well as the steady rise in the number of banks opening their first overseas unit. US institutions have led this surge; from roughly 100 offices in 1951, the number of foreign branches of US banks had risen to 730 at the end of 1977.[2] Whereas one bank accounted for well over half of the US branches in 1964, and three had over 100 each at the end of 1977, a total of 130 US banks operated overseas branches at that latter date.[3]

Banks from other countries have responded to this challenge. British banks have moved in the 1970s away from their traditional dependence on semi-autonomous affiliates to acquire control of existing overseas banks and set up new branches, while German institutions, after losing their extensive international network on two occasions after World Wars, have begun once again to rebuild these organisations. Whereas only three German overseas branches existed at the end of 1963, a total of 46 branches and 35 subsidiaries were in operation by the end of 1977.[4] Similar overseas growth has been shown by banks in France, Japan and other major Western countries.

The impact of this remarkable international expansion is reflected in the available data showing the extent of foreign penetration of individual national banking markets. By 1978, the roughly 100 foreign banks active in the US accounted for significant shares of the banking markets in the key states of California, Illinois and New York. In the latter state, for

TABLE 3.2 Breakdown of Claims of Banks Against Non-residents, 1974–7 (amounts in $ billions, as of 31 December)

Claims of:	1974		1975		1976		1977	
	Amount	% of total	Amount	% of total	Amount	% of total	Amount	% of total
1. Banks in the US	46.2	12	59.8	13	80.8	14	89.6	14
2. Banks in the UK[1]	102.6	28	118.2	26	138.4	25	159.9	24
3. Banks in Ten Countries[2] (foreign currency)	147.1	40	174.1	39	206.5	37	254.4	38
4. Banks in Nine Countries[3] (domestic currency)	31.6	8	39.2	9	47.7	9	59.8	9
5. Caribbean Area	31.7	9	45.2	10	66.8	12	80.0	12
6. Asian Dollar Market	10.4	3	12.6	3	17.4	3	20.5	3
GRAND TOTAL[4]	369.6	100	449.1	100	557.6	100	664.2	100
of which: US banks and their overseas branches	198.1	54	236.3	53	300.0	54	349.6	53

1. Foreign currency position only.
2. Banks in Luxembourg, Belgium, France, Germany, Italy, Netherlands, Sweden, Switzerland, Canada and Japan.
3. Banks in first eight countries mentioned in (2) above plus UK.
4. Includes substantial interbank positions between areas.

Sources: David Llewellyn, *Trends in International Banking and Capital Markets*, as derived from Federal Reserve Bulletin, B.I.S. Press Release, Bank of England Quarterly Bulletin.

example, the share of foreign offices in the commercial and industrial loans outstanding in May 1978 was 43.4 per cent, whereas in November 1972 the extent of penetration was only 23.2 per cent.[5] Conversely, in the UK, American bank branches and subsidiaries at the end of 1977 accounted for 10 per cent of sterling advances to UK residents.[6]

A final indication of the increased importance of international business to domestic banks is given by Figure 3.1 which traces the growth of domestic and international lending of banks in Germany and the US. Such statistics have been selected not only because of the key role played in the Euro-markets by these banks, but also because of the relative quality of information produced in these two countries.

What has been more unexpected is the movement overseas of non-US banks, many of whom vowed as late as the mid-1970s that they did not need branches abroad, that the Euro-currency market was unreliable and unstable, and that they had no interest in doing business internationally with any but their existing domestic customers. A growing number of national banks, therefore, has come to regard the international market as a desirable target in its own right. While their natural preference is for a domestic or existing customer, they are now prepared to look at international lending opportunities on their own merits and not simply as an appendage of their basic domestic business. As a result, the international market has reached a level of self-sustaining growth which includes an element of self-fulfilling prophecy, because as more banks develop purely international operations in anticipation of a growth in this market, the latter in fact does grow, if only because the new entrants have made their contribution. Whether a new representative office or branch, the physical opening of a new business development outlet creates significant human and institutional pressures for that office to add new business for the group.

CHARACTERISTIC FEATURES

As the Euro-currency market has grown since the early 1970s, the portion of its asset base represented by sovereign risk exposure has increased significantly. This trend away from the

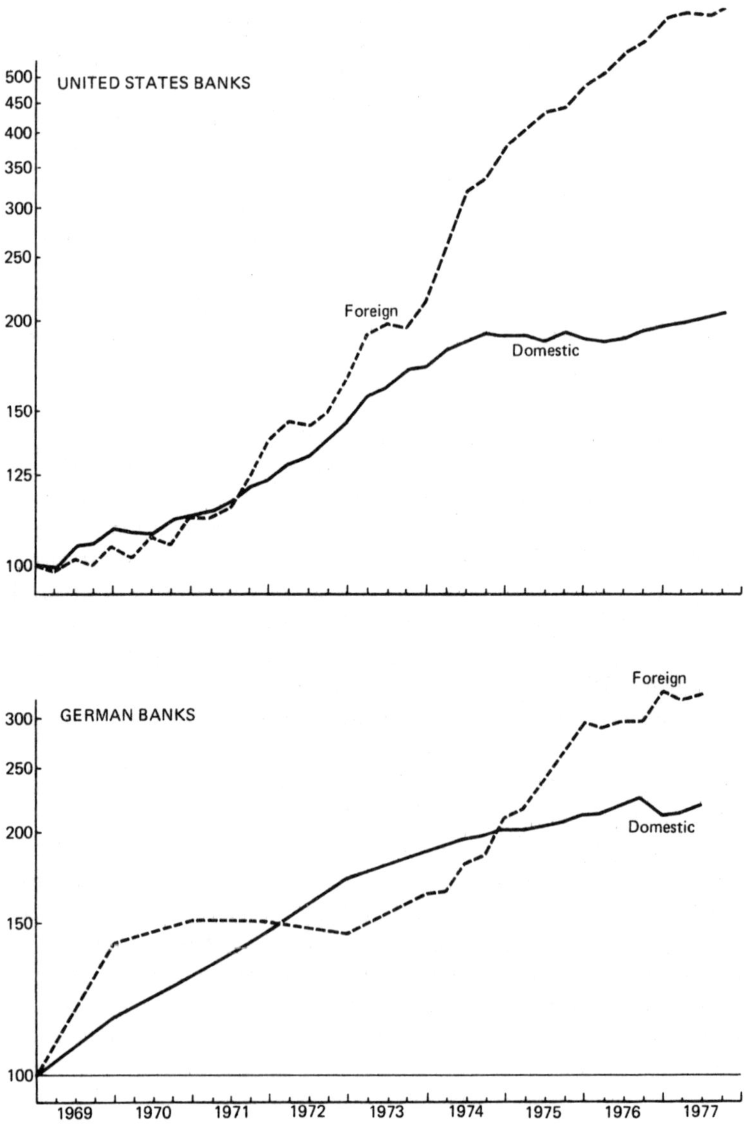

FIGURE 3.1 Domestic and External Lending of Banks in Germany and the United States (1968(4)=100)

Source: David Llewellyn, *Trends in International Banking and Capital Markets.*

corporate lending which represented the original impetus to the market is difficult to quantify, in particular since many loans carry both a sovereign and corporate credit risk, but Table 3.3 provides some indications of this trend.

TABLE 3.3 Net Exposure (assets less liabilities) of Banks in Group of Ten countries and Switzerland towards Specific Borrowing Countries (amounts in $ billions)

Country	12/31/74	12/31/77	% increase over three years
Brazil	3.802	16.540	335
Mexico	3.240	13.507	317
South Africa	2.197	6.373	190
USSR	0.074	6.332	8457
Poland	1.669	6.407	284
Denmark	1.180	5.504	366
Sweden	0.140	4.518	3127
Norway	0.518	3.600	595
Spain	(3.992)	3.122	INF
Finland	1.199	2.988	149
Peru	0.653	2.513	285
South Korea	1.135	2.227	96
Turkey	(0.646)	1.983	INF
Net grand total of above countries	$11.169	$75.614	577%

The 13 countries in Table 3.3 to whom international banks' exposure has more than doubled in three years have been selected for this reason rather than any perceived level of credit risk, although clearly the great bulk of them represent a different level of risk from that of the Group of Ten countries in which the Euro-currency market originated. The aggregate exposure of international banks to these countries increased by 577 per cent in the three years up to 1977 while the overall Euro-currency market as reflected in Table 3.2 only grew by 80 per cent over the same period. While there has been a massive shift in the nature of international lending towards sovereign borrowers, diversification of risk continues to limit banks' exposure to individual sovereign borrowers. At the end of 1977, for example, loans to Eastern European borrowers represented only 5 per cent of claims by banks in the Group of Ten countries, while exposure to Brazil accounted for only 3.5 per cent of the banks' global commitments.

The greater relative importance of loans to sovereign entities reflects the increased lending capacity in the market as much as it does the relative financial requirements of multinational as opposed to sovereign borrowers. The latter tend to have sizeable permanent potential requirements, as opposed to private corporations whose needs are regulated by profit considerations, and it would appear that the loan demand on the part of newcomers to the market has only been accommodated by the requirements of the sovereign borrowers.

A dominant feature of today's Euro-currency market is its efficiency in the broadest sense of the term. This efficiency is reflected in a positive sense in the ability of an acceptable bank in normal times to raise fairly substantial sums from other banks in a matter of minutes at market rates. In addition, the technique of marginal pricing through the use of the London Interbank Offered Rate for given maturities eliminates for the lender the possible squeeze in margins which can occur with the use of an administered rate subject to political influence such as Base Rate in the UK and prime rate in the US. As will be discussed subsequently, management may choose not to match its loan rollover and deposit periods, but in normal circumstances the lender does not have to take an interest rate risk on his loan portfolio.

Other variables in the lending function have either been eliminated or reduced to standard formulae. While Euro-currency loan agreements can provoke a few violent arguments, the points at issue are usually few and far between. With few exceptions, therefore, the key variables in negotiating a Euro-currency loan have been reduced to maturity and pricing. The variable of currency, for example, has been controlled by covenants limiting the borrower's option to currencies such as dollars, Deutschemarks and Swiss Francs which can be raised fairly easily from the deposit or foreign exchange markets. Non-US banks have traditionally been concerned about their ability to attract dollar deposits to fund Euro-currency loans, but overall market liquidity since 1974 plus the proliferation of foreign branches and agencies in the US would appear to have significantly alleviated this potential problem.

By potentially limiting such variables, however, this efficient market has led to an increasingly homogeneous and well-defined product, which in turn has resulted in a more intense level of competition than would have been the case with more product differentiation. On the lending side, the great majority of syndicated loans—principally sovereign risk credits—are marketed to participants essentially by telex, which presumes a fairly straightforward yes-or-no credit decision; only rarely does a bank's credit function have to pile through reams of statistics to sort out the risks involved. Loan terms are precisely defined by a highly efficient pricing mechanism; for most borrowers at any given time in the market, the informed lender can immediately quote the 'right' maturity and loan spread, give or take $\frac{1}{8}$ per cent in rate or a year in maturity.

This relative lack of product differentiation intensifies the existing degree of competition which stems from the steady increase in the number of market participants and the growing pressure on them to show continued growth in international earnings and assets. With several hundred international banks looking for business, it is much easier to cut prices on a standardised product than it would be for a specialist one where only a limited number of competitors are prepared to understand and bid for the business. The oft-mentioned tendency for Euro-lending to swing naturally towards a borrower's market thus reflects a combination of an increasingly homogeneous product and a larger number of participants interested in increasing their international exposure.

Another by-product of the efficiency of the market of vital interest to management is the crucial question of confidence. This characteristic is, of course, by definition an integral factor throughout the world in the banking sector; virtually no level of liquidity or capitalisation will protect a bank from its depositors if, rightly or wrongly, they are convinced that their obligor is unsound.

This is even more true of Euro-banking, where a greater portion of deposits is obtained from the potentially more volatile money market than is the case domestically, and where rumours can spread with the speed of a telephone call. Moreover, the time disparity between final loan maturity and average life of deposit—and, therefore, the potential liquidity gap—is perhaps higher in the Euro-currency market than in any other. This so-called transformation of short-term deposits into long-term loans is clearly one of the structural weaknesses of the international markets.

The crisis of confidence which struck the international banking community in 1974 after the Franklin and Herstatt failures came very close to a domino-like collapse of the Euro-currency market by cutting off the supply of funds to smaller and newer banks, which in turn could have led to a broader freezing of assets and liabilities. Given this market characteristic and the absence of an agreed international lender of last resort, it is understandable that international bank management does everything in its power to maintain its market reputation as well as secure backstop funding arrangements. For a period of time in 1974, a variety of otherwise viable banks were faced with the choice of funding their loan book with shorter maturities than they would have wished, paying a premium rate for funds or using the backstop funding facilities of parent or related institutions. While the 1974 crisis passed—in part because of firm action by the Bank of England with regard to UK-based affiliates of foreign banks—the nature of the market is such that there is no guarantee against a recurrence of such a crisis in the future.

Another reflection of the efficiency of communications in the market is the tendency of international banks to imitate the behaviour of those regarded as leaders. Whether it involves a new organisational structure, setting up in a new financial centre, or developing a specialist expertise or product, one can be certain of a wave of imitators as the market followers struggle to keep up with the innovators. Once a newcomer to the ranks of international borrowers is accepted in the form of a successfully placed loan, he can be sure of receiving the visits of a variety of bankers who had studiously ignored him previously. By the same token, if word gets around that a market leader has a negative view on a particular sovereign borrower, the latter will have some explaining to do to anxious lenders to maintain its name in the market.

OTHER EXTERNAL CHALLENGES FOR THE INTERNATIONAL BANKER

The challenges to management represented by the evolution of the Euro-markets are only a few of the variety posed by external factors in the international banking market of the late 1970s. One of those with the most direct impact on international banks is the appearance of the multinational corporation with a highly centralised and sophisticated financial management, specialised requirements throughout the world and often a sizeable appetite for funds in a variety of currencies. Quite apart from the need to protect an existing relationship from the depredations of competitor institutions, banks have found that the level of financial expertise represented by these clients is often equal to or superior to that of their own international banking officers, who are more at home in dealing with other bank or sovereign institutions. Moreover, the often centralised approach to financial decision-making in these firms places at a disadvantage banks organised on a territorial basis with an account officer who may or may not have an understanding of international finance.

A second challenge is the total revolution in credit assessment procedures represented by the movement towards sovereign risk borrowers taking up historically large amounts of funds for what to lenders are unprecedented maturities. For international bankers accustomed to short-term, self-liquidating, trade-related transactions, evaluating the ability and willingness of a sovereign borrower ten years hence to meet its foreign currency obligations is at best an uncomfortable task. Substantial efforts have been made by individual banks to rank and quantify risks utilising the limited availability of published data, and banks have focused on financing individual projects with identifiable cash flows as a partial compensation for the uncertainties involved in sovereign lending. On balance, however, most bankers resort to rough generalisations in evaluating country risk and feel distinctly out of their element with such risks.

Another challenge is the heightened importance of a bank's capital base as the result of inflation, pressures from regulatory authorities, competition, domestic losses and other factors. While many nationalised or other well-established national banks place relatively little emphasis on capital adequacy and the need to earn an attractive return on capital, for most banks this is one of the critical issues faced by management. In countries such as the US and UK with highly sophisticated capital markets and strong regulatory authorities, growth and market position can only be sustained by an earnings record which builds the capital base through retained earnings and supports a stock market valuation which permits additional capital to be raised on satisfactory terms. Since the recession of 1974–5, earnings growth from domestic sources has been minimal or unsatisfactory in most major national markets, which has placed on the international function the burden of maintaining the overall steady earnings growth desired by investors and other constituencies. The global impact of competition on gross margins and of inflation on costs has not only depressed absolute levels of bank earnings around the world, but also made it that much more difficult to achieve returns on assets and capital considered appropriate by regulatory authorities and investors.

A final challenge is the growing complexity of factors with which an international management must deal in the normal course of business. Regulatory authorities are responding to international expansion with greater reporting requirements, operating guidelines and exchange controls to regulate currency flows which inevitably involve a considerable portion of management time. Operating an overseas network requires balancing the respective claims of a host of foreign and domestic tax, regulatory, compensation, allocation of resources, physical premises, staff transfer and internal audit requirements. The management information and accounting system needed to execute a growing volume of transactions, monitor performance and assist management in its decision-making process represents both a high degree of sophistication and an additional learning challenge for management. In short, the senior international banker who achieved his position by virtue of performance in lending money successfully or developing new business, is now required to spend an increasing portion of his time as a manager rather than banker. The balance of the book will explore how he has reacted to these management challenges.

4 Objectives and Strategy

The objectives established for the international function of a bank and the strategy devised to achieve these objectives are clearly the starting point for an analysis of the management function of individual banking institutions. 'Objectives', for definitional purposes, refer to goals which are desirable in themselves, while 'strategy' refers to the broad measures an individual bank takes to achieve these goals. The two are frequently confused in that strategic measures are mistakenly taken for objectives.

The purpose of this chapter is, therefore, to describe first how and to what extent banks have articulated their long term international objectives and, secondly, the various strategic options devised to implement such objectives. From the theory and practice of setting objectives and strategy flow the other principal chapter topics of this book—marketing, asset and liability management, network development, organisational structure and performance measurement.[1]

EVOLUTION OF THE INTERNATIONAL BANKING FUNCTION

To place this key topic in its proper perspective, however, one must describe first the evolution of the typical international banking function as it has responded to the external challenges outlined in Chapter 3. While there are obviously many deviations from the pattern described below, and while factors such as a bank's size and level of international sophistication have a major impact on the timing and form of this evolution, the broad outline of this evolutionary process is typical of most banks which are active in the international market today. Quite clearly a bank with a long history of international business through, perhaps, old colonial ties, has a different perspective from the institution which is the principal focus of this book, namely the national or domestic bank which has developed its main international impetus since World War II.

In its original state—which in calendar terms could extend as far back as the 1950s—the international function of a national bank was a service department responding fairly passively to the needs of domestic and overseas customers and representing a very minor portion of the bank's overall staffing, assets and earnings. Services offered normally related to trade finance—collections, letters of credit, the provision of foreign exchange—and overseas customers tended to be primarily foreign banks with whom correspondent relationships in individual overseas countries were established. The human skills required at this stage of a bank's international development were those of a generalist and diplomat as well as technical knowledge of foreign trade transactions and the movement of funds internationally. In its role as a passive service organisation dealing primarily with other banks, the international function was thus usually well removed from the mainstream of a bank's corporate deposit and lending operations. Organisationally, because of this factor and the relatively small profit contribution made by his function, the head of international was rarely a key member of his bank's senior management team. While the appellation of 'Foreign' or 'International' Department was clearly a geographic designation, in most European and other banks it was effectively a functional one as well in that it provided specialist services rather than operating as a 'bank within a bank'.

Typically the first evolutionary step away from this prototype was the initiation of certain service functions in response to the explicit needs of domestic corporate customers. While a foreign exchange function may have existed in the form of a correspondent nostro (own account) balance which could be used to meet a customer's currency requirements, a new dealing function might be set up to operate directly in the market and, in addition, take currency positions for the bank's own account. The need to diversify or expand sources of money market deposits for essentially domestic purposes—particularly in countries with controls on domestic lending—would lead to the establishment of an initial foreign branch or subsidiary, often a 'brass plate' operation which functioned with little or no autonomy as a funding arm of the parent organisation.

Having established its bank's name in the Euro-currency markets as a taker of deposits primarily for domestic purposes, an obvious next step was trading deposits to earn matched and mismatched profits on the interbank or redeposit book. Another approach might involve participation as a minority partner in a consortium of hopefully like-minded institutions to test the international water and minimise the commitment of staff and other resources.

Until this point a bank's international function still revolved primarily around relationships with other banks. With the overseas expansion of domestic corporate customers and the implantation locally of foreign corporations, the international function had to deal to an increasing extent with the creditworthiness, sophistication and operating techniques associated with what have come to be known as multinational corporations. To a certain extent, this evolution posed no serious problems to the international function as maturities were short, transactions self-liquidating and the credit that of the domestic parent who was known to the bank's domestic lending function, or a foreign banking correspondent who would guarantee its corporate customer. Increasingly, however, credit exposure came to involve term maturities, the absence of a domestic parent guarantee and the assumption of a foreign country or corporate risk with which the bank had had little or no experience.

Concurrently, there arose the question of whether to continue to work through foreign bank correspondents or to solicit the growing and profitable multinational business directly. Banks which had established or developed an initial branch for funding purposes in a major financial centre such as London found that an aggressive business development approach to local corporations, coupled with the use of relatively new techniques such as term lending, could attract profitable local business to supplement earnings from the funding operations. Abandoning the traditional correspondent relationships as a source of new business, a number of American banks, therefore, moved more aggressively into major national markets such as Germany, France and Japan by establishing new branches and other offices with the objectives of attracting new business from domestic and foreign corporations as well as broadening their funding base. In this process of physically expanding abroad, local managers explored new market possibilities: profitable funding from the local currency interbank market, diversification outside traditional wholesale banking operations, and increased profits from the trading of foreign exchange and Euro-currencies.

The pattern described above is essentially that of the larger American money centre and regional banks which have shaped the Euro-currency market as it is today—with their currency, their language and their lending practices in the forefront. But the same rough pattern of internal responses to these external challenges has been shown in the 1970s by non-American institutions. In answer, for example, to the challenge posed by foreign banks actively soliciting their traditional domestic corporate business, as well as the apparent profitability of overseas operations, branch networks outside their national market began to be established by European and other banks which had previously seen no advantage to branching abroad.

The management challenge of operating a new overseas network was further complicated by the growth in importance of country risk lending on a large scale to relatively untested sovereign borrowers and diversification into new sectors such as merchant/investment banking and retail banking abroad, all of which required new credit and management skills. From a relatively passive, service-oriented stance, the international banking function had moved in a few years to one involving highly sophisticated credit skills; a complex management information and control system, along with a data processing function to handle an enormous increase in volume; a significant use of the bank's balance sheet resources; and the contribution of a growing portion of the bank's revenues. The successful management of a growing network of overseas offices, an active business development function focused on multinational and sovereign risk clients, as well as an active interbank foreign-exchange and deposit book operated from a variety of overseas offices obviously requires a level of staff expertise in personnel, data processing, marketing, planning and economic analysis which was totally unnecessary before.

Within individual banks, the growth of the international function created a number of stresses. From a customer relations standpoint, international officers wanted access to corporate customers traditionally serviced by the bank's domestic divisions, and solutions had to be found to reconcile these historical and personal relationships with the need to respond to the customer's requirements on a global basis. From a personnel standpoint, the human skills needed to solicit and service corporate customers internationally as well as run often sizeable overseas operations could most easily be found in the bank's domestic functions, so that arrangements had to be made to allocate scarce human resources between the domestic and international functions. Also, the increasing percentage of a bank's resources pre-empted by the international function, particularly in countries where balance sheet leverage represented a real constraint on growth, raised the obvious questions of whether an adequate return was being realised on international assets and whether the bank's traditional identity would be lost through an excessive increase in international business.

Finally, from a subjective standpoint, domestic resentments may have arisen as a result of the relative inexperience of international officers, the glamour of international banking and the management attention devoted to this function, while on the other hand, international officers may have resented the apparent unwillingness of a domestic relationship officer to share this relationship for the benefit of the bank as a whole. To a large extent these problems have been alleviated by greater communications and internal transfer of bank officers, but the issue of 'two banks' remains a difficult one. In describing the relationship in large American banks between these two functions, one observer refers to international departments which 'have resembled networks of feudal duchies rather than well-integrated business areas'.[2] A senior American banker summarised the problems facing management by explaining that 'the problem with all banks' international activities is the fact that when they grew internationally, they very rightly grew in a separate compartment of the bank. In all large institutions the domestic and international areas have become very large—and in most cases rather independent of each other—whereas the corporate world has become very closely linked together.'[3]

Banks active internationally thus find themselves somewhere in the evolutionary continuum between the prototype bank offering as a passive service function a limited number of trade financing services and, at the other extreme, a truly universal bank making available a wide range of investment and commercial banking services through a network of units which literally covers the globe. Movement along this evolutionary scale—in both directions—is stimulated by such factors as the relative attractiveness of domestic business, availability of qualified staff, actual experience in the international market, the perception of client requirements and the availability of physical resources. A bank with total assets of $1 billion equivalent obviously finds it difficult to move in the direction of a universal international bank, but even a bank twenty times its size must resolve the same problems of availability of human resources, the usual preference of senior management for the domestic business with which they have been familiar, questions of relative profitability of domestic versus international business and the need to compete effectively in a market not significantly characterised by product differentiation.

THE SETTING OF OBJECTIVES

It is in this evolutionary context which banks today establish their long-term objectives. In the 40-bank survey whose methodology was outlined in Chapter 1, it was apparent that relatively few banks have elaborated and communicated internally a well-thought-out set of international objectives ranked in terms of priority. Profitability and service to customers are the two most frequently cited objectives, a ranking which reflects the increasing profit orientation of banks throughout the world as well as the oft-expressed view that banks are in business primarily to service their customers' requirements.

Of the 33 banks in the survey which were prepared to express a priority, roughly three-quarters stress profits, while for the remaining quarter servicing existing or new customers is the top priority. A slightly higher percentage—80 per cent—of the North American banks cited profits as their principal objective; only 58 per cent of the other institutions took the same view. The same emphasis on profitability is reflected by cumulating the top three objectives expressed by the bankers. Profitability and service to customers were cited by all but a few banks as two of their three principal objectives. In quantifying their profit objectives, most banks refer to a target percentage of total bank earnings or portion of the balance sheet represented by international business. Interestingly enough, less than one-third of all the banks interviewed felt that meeting competition was one of these three top priorities. A few banks believe that furthering their country's national interests is a valid priority objective, while others referred to improving the quality of service, increasing the extent of diversification, maintaining market share, and providing a full range of services.

In some of these cases, it can be argued that strategies are being confused with objectives. Many, for example, pointed out that effective servicing of customer requirements permits banks to achieve their profit objectives and that the two are inextricably linked together in the real world. It can also be argued that such objectives, which are generally incorporated in some form of annual planning process, do not necessarily reflect the actual priorities pursued in practice. Profit maximisation is undoubtedly a very real objective for virtually all banks, but the relative importance of service to customers as an *objective* can be disputed. While the provision of banking services which are hopefully of high quality and reflect a relatively unique approach is undoubtedly of great importance to international bankers, this presumed objective is often articulated to the outside world as an acceptable justification for a decision which is motivated in reality by other objectives such as profitability, diversification of risk, expansion of market share, etc.

Responding to competitive pressures and increasing market share are, on the other hand, goals which are often cloaked under what are assumed to be more acceptable objectives. Banks which, for example, have the largest single share of a given national banking market are unlikely to broadcast the fact that one of their principal objectives in expanding internationally is to retain that prized position. Recognition of reality is also a factor in the setting of priorities; one US bank has deliberately established customer service as its top priority as it recognises that in the current market it cannot demonstrate superior profit performance to the domestic banking function. Another rarely articulated but highly relevant objective is the offsetting of domestic profit shortfalls. Many banks plagued with unexciting domestic earnings—or, worse, significant domestic loan losses—have deliberately used international business as an accordion or buffer to offset these shortfalls; when domestic earnings recover, correspondingly less emphasis is placed on international business.

Although most bankers have thus established profitability

and service as long-term objectives, relatively few institutions communicate them throughout their organisation and attempt to quantify or articulate them in the type of detail which lends itself to an effective overall planning process. American, Canadian and British banks are fairly specific about their profit and other objectives, whereas at the other extreme, Japanese and Southern European institutions tend to rely on implicit, fairly general statements of objectives.

There is some degree of correlation, however, between the relative importance of the international function and the specificity of objectives. Large American banks, for example, have relatively well articulated objectives, but it can also be assumed that other institutions come under considerable internal and external pressure to justify their use of resources when the latter approaches one third or more of total assets or income. In such circumstances long-term profitability is perhaps the most logical justification for the claim on resources, whereas in a small or less internationally-oriented institution, a relatively implicit, defensive commitment to serve existing customers will suffice as a *raison d'être* for the international function. For banks such as US regional and Japanese institutions, however, as the international function expands considerably to provide such services, incremental profitability is increasingly called upon to justify the substantial commitment of resources.

THE DETERMINATION OF STRATEGY

The essential components of a strategy designed to achieve a given set of objectives involve the definition of customer profile, the appropriate mix and focus of services offered, geographic emphasis, risk preference and character of network of offices. In a market where the basic product is undifferentiated—money—and where several hundred banks offer roughly the same services, such a strategy essentially involves establishing an appropriate mix of these factors which will enable the bank to achieve its acknowledged primary objectives of profitability and service.

In establishing its customer profile, a bank can select target clients by size (large multinationals versus smaller, middle-market firms), industry sector (e.g. energy, transportation, automobile), level of sophistication (OECD-based firms versus those in developing countries), type of requirement (trade financing, buyer credits, project financing, etc.) and type of ownership (private versus public, individual versus corporate). In terms of services offered, a bank can consider diversification beyond the traditional lending and deposit services offered (into investment or merchant banking, finance-related services such as leasing or factoring, or non-financial services such as tourism or consulting), the relative emphasis on quality (a personalised and highly efficient clearing service as opposed to one which simply fills out a product line), the extent of traditional banking services offered (is it desirable to offer services which are not profitable or competitive simply to have a full range of products) and the relative focus on retail as opposed to wholesale business. Inevitably, in defining its product strategy a bank will emphasise those factors related to its domestic market position and network skills—for example, the largest Japanese bank or an institution with the most extensive branch network in a given region.

In building a strategy around a geographic profile, an international bank must first determine the extent to which it will rely on overseas offices to market its services as opposed to home office-based marketing. If a major emphasis is to be placed on the former, decisions must be made as to which countries or regions will have priority: major international money centres, countries with substantial internal markets, or particular regions of the world in which the bank feels comfortable and which have perceived growth and profit potential. To the extent that the bank plans to focus on a limited number of markets and may attempt to achieve a significant share in those markets, the issue of possible over-concentration and subsequent vulnerability must be considered.

The issue of risk preference is vital in elaborating an international strategy. While in its early growth phases a significant return could be obtained without an equivalent degree of risk, the growing maturity and competitiveness of the international banking market has severely limited these opportunities. Risk in this context is defined not only to include the possibility of asset losses but also the risk taken in running foreign exchange and deposit mismatch positions. The traditional importance attached to banking conservatism and safety makes it difficult for many international bankers to admit that they can and should take deliberate risks in running these positions and managing their asset portfolio. It is quite valid as a strategic option, however, to structure a relatively risky loan portfolio through a focus on types of clients or a specific level of concentration, and to rely on one's expertise and the higher return associated with this type of portfolio to minimise and absorb the higher losses which might result. Whether individual bankers are prepared to admit it or not, the running of a foreign exchange or deposit mismatched position as well as lending to a heavily borrowed developing country does, in fact, reflect a conscious choice of risk and reward.

Finally, if the bank is to operate a network of any size as part of its strategy, the character of this network must be defined. Recognising that a bank's strategic needs may change over time, it is still necessary to define the extent to which the network will be responsive to home office requirements and contribute to the bank's identity abroad; whether the network will focus on wholesale or retail business; whether the additional management and financial commitment of a branch or subsidiary as against a representative office is justified, and whether the bank has the necessary resources to run the desired network. From such analysis should emerge the appropriate mix of participation in consortia or joint ventures, branches, subsidiaries and representative offices, as well as the physical size of the network.

From all these factors should emerge a personality or image expressed in terms of the bank's strategy. It is this style—e.g. small and flexible, big and competitive, conservative or aggressive—which will be the basis for the bank's ability to differentiate itself sufficiently in a highly competitive market to achieve its stated objectives.

While senior bankers have in one form or another addressed each of these aspects of strategy formulation in the process of developing their international business, it is relatively rare to find a thoroughgoing and comprehensive strategy established at the outset of a bank's international development. More typically, a bank has simply responded to such specific challenges and opportunities as a competitive threat, a profit opportunity, the leadership of an aggressive member of senior management or the international department, the demands of traditional customers and the need to be seen to be active in a growing market populated by competitors. As the size and profitability of the international function grows, more systematic efforts are usually made to define specifically where the bank is going internationally and how it will get there.

To a very large extent, the relative lack of strategic thinking in a bank's early expansionary phase reflects both the background of senior international bankers and the traditions which have, until fairly recently, characterised the banking industry. Until the 1960s when a few American banks began to regard their business as simply another industry whose ultimate objective was to maximise long term profitability to the stockholders, banking was a heavily regulated, utility-type sector which existed to safeguard customer deposits, intermediate these deposits into secure, self-liquidating and high quality loans and fixed rate investments, maintain sufficient liquidity to meet depositors' needs, and provide the banking services required by retail, corporate and government clients. Relations with other banks tended to be co-operative rather than competitive, and management success tended to be measured in terms of quality of assets and service as well as continuity and reliability. The relative focus in many countries since the mid to late 1960s on profitability as the ultimate goal of the bank has obviously upset this pattern, and international banking with its relative newness and its significant profit potential has particularly felt the resulting emphasis on competition, profit performance, need to establish an identity and differentiate products and other factors which were relatively unimportant in earlier years.

International bank management itself has reflected this transformation of objectives, style and performance criteria. Traditionally, senior international bankers had risen in the corporate hierarchy on the basis of proficiency and success in dealing with other banks, in providing a specialised service such as foreign exchange or in general knowledge of the international scene. With the new emphasis on profits and the need to compete to obtain these profits, other skills assumed greater importance: corporate lending experience, skill in creating and marketing new products, management information and data processing expertise, and the personnel skills needed to manage a multinational staff throughout the world became vital considerations. Perhaps most important were the management skills required to organise and direct this rapidly evolving and growing international structure.

SPECIFIC STRATEGIC APPROACHES

The responses by senior international bank managers in mid-1978 to questions relating to strategy thus reflect in many cases a transitional phase between acceptance of the more traditional modes of behaviour and a more articulated and detailed approach to achieving profit and other objectives. Of the 25 banks responding to the specific question, speed/flexibility of the decision-making process and specialist expertise were each mentioned by about one-quarter of the banks as representing the single most important facet of their long-term strategy. Another quarter mentioned quality of service or unique products and services as their highest priority strategic element, so that if one assumes that quality of service is equivalent to a specialist function, the largest number of banks, roughly one-half, focus on some form of product or service differentiation as their principal competitive weapon. No other specific strategic approach was mentioned by more than 15 per cent of the bankers.

If one evaluates these responses by combining the three highest priorities ranked by the respondents, speed/flexibility of decision-making was by far the most frequently mentioned competitive strategy (by 28 banks). Another 17 banks gave specialist expertise as one of the top priorities, 16 mentioned the existence of a large existing customer base and 13 cited the ability to commit relatively large amounts of funds. If one lumps together those citing specialist/unique/high quality expertise, the resulting figure of 27 banks is comparable to the number focusing on speed/flexibility of response. The most significant difference in response between North American and other banks is the relative emphasis by non-US and Canadian institutions on the priority of a large existing customer base. This would appear to reflect the relatively defensive objectives of many European and other banks in protecting their customer base from the assault of US institutions and the latters' relative lack in many cases of such a base.

At the risk of over-generalising, therefore, it would appear that the typical international bank defines its strategy in terms of finding some degree of product or service differentiation and emphasising its ability to provide a quick and constructive response to customer requirements. In practical terms, banks look to their natural strengths—domestic industry, geographic location, market share, existing services—to 'find a niche' or otherwise differentiate themselves from their competitors. Larger banks can be expected to explore market opportunities on a fairly thoroughgoing and comprehensive basis to select their targets and priorities, whereas smaller institutions tend to rely on existing skills and specialities to achieve the desired level of differentiation. As will be discussed in a subsequent chapter, however, customers may well disagree both as to the responsiveness of the decision-making process and the extent to which a given bank's services are truly unique or superior to those of the competition.

Of almost equal interest are the possible competitive strategies which ranked lowest in the respondents' priorities. Only five banks, for example, mentioned fineness or competitiveness of pricing as one of their three priority competitive elements. This reflects traditional attitudes towards the use of pricing as a competitive factor; few banks want to see themselves as deliberate price cutters. In the real competitive world, however, such a strategic element is often necessary for survival, as is emphasised in the level of loan spreads in mid-1978 as well as the responses given by chief financial officers as described in a subsequent chapter. The priority given by so many banks to the responsiveness of their decision-making process might well reflect a desideratum or objective, more than a strategic means, in view of the widespread criticism, particularly of the larger banks, as to the time necessary to receive approval for a given commitment.

Another possible competitive factor which received relatively little emphasis is the offering of unique products and services, which was mentioned as a priority by only six institutions. The vast majority of the bankers interviewed were quite pessimistic about their ability to introduce and profit from such new products in view of the highly competitive nature of the market and the difficulty of developing a product or service which was truly innovative.

Banks outside the US were those who placed a particularly high priority on their ability to commit large amounts of funds and on the possession of a large existing customer base. Once again, at the risk of over-generalising, a typical European or Japanese bank would appear to place a great deal of strategic emphasis on its ability to commit large amounts of funds on an expeditious basis for an existing customer which it knew well. American banks, on the other hand, seem to rely more on product differentiation and the geographic coverage of their world-wide network as well as the speed and flexibility of their decision-making process to win business.

Another factor in the setting of strategy is the relative urgency of pressure to achieve given objectives. Banks which have a substantial amount of natural business stemming from their location or historical ties, or who effectively control the business of their domestic customers, naturally have less incentive to elaborate a detailed strategic plan involving significant product differentiation. There is also an understandably high degree of correlation between the size of an institution and its relative emphasis on breadth of product line and geographic coverage of the market. The very largest banks naturally tend to compete on the basis of their ability to offer all (or most) things to all people, whereas those with limited resources must necessarily specialise.

The extent of diversification of services is a significant issue in strategy determination. The issue generally focuses around the relative desirability of going beyond traditional commercial banking services to the investment banking sector (Euro-bond underwriting and dealing, investment management, the arrangement of Euro-currency loans, private placements and mergers and acquisitions) or to such finance-related services as leasing, factoring and consulting. For institutions whose local regulations and market traditions have permitted such diversification, it is accepted as a totally natural and desirable state of affairs. In countries such as the US, Japan, Canada and the UK where this is not the case, there is a general desire in principle to enter these non-traditional sectors in order to earn the off-balance sheet income needed to supplement interest differential earnings and provide a broader range of customer services.

Of the 39 banks responding to the question, therefore, only 6, or 15 per cent of the total, felt that diversification beyond the commercial banking sector was not particularly desirable. All but one of the non-North American banks interviewed supported the universal banking concept, while three-quarters of the US and Canadian institutions, which are restrained domestically from investment banking activities, agreed. On the other hand, the rationale and strength of feeling among the latter banks varied considerably. Some expressed a very lukewarm, experimental, in principle, desire to expand their range of services and were clearly uncomfortable in doing so. Many were frank to admit that their rationale for expanding into investment banking activities was either purely defensive or motivated by the need to exploit another market now that their traditional sector of activity had become so competitive. By the same token, those with relatively undeveloped domestic or international commercial banking potential were correspondingly unexcited by the glittering prospects of fee earnings from investment banking services. The very largest banks without an investment banking tradition, however, tended to be the greatest advocates of diversification, given their objective of maximum market coverage.

Of the institutions which expressed a desire to go beyond commercial banking services, the sector of investment or merchant banking was of interest to 25, while for 22 banks such bank-related services as leasing and factoring have some priority. Among the larger US banks, the issue is not whether to offer investment banking services, but how to organise themselves internally for such a market opportunity. Organisational responses from these institutions range from a few relatively autonomous, separately capitalised entities located in major financial centres such as London, to a larger number of non-autonomous but separately incorporated institutions in a city such as London or Hong Kong which group the bank's investment banking personnel and functions, to a few departmental operations based in home office which provide the same expertise to the bank and its clients. For institutions such as large commercial banks, the disruption to organisational structures and procedures represented by a group of presumably high-performance, relatively autonomous specialists is a greater problem than the difficulty of attracting and retaining the high-potential individuals who are essential to investment banking success. In many cases, US banks have combined their domestic specialists in investment banking activities, such as private placements, with their international equivalents, not only to better serve their global customers, but also to maximise the transfer of expertise.

5 The Management Processes and Organisational Structure

Having determined its objectives and strategy, the international bank must next establish the organisational structure and management processes which best reflect these factors as well as a variety of others. This chapter will describe, therefore, how an international function actually operates: how it is structured, how decisions are made, how key line and staff functions relate to each other, and how their processes and structures evolve in line with a bank's perceived needs.

TYPES OF ORGANISATIONAL ORIENTATION

Broadly speaking, an organisational structure in international banking can be oriented along three different lines: product or function, geography and customer. In most cases, structures are built around two or sometimes three of these focal points.

A product/functional orientation relates to specific services offered by the bank: money dealing, export finance, lending in general, capital market activities, correspondent banking services, mergers and acquisitions, and the like. Specific internally-oriented services such as planning, data processing and marketing are also essentially organised on a product basis. Such a service-oriented structure facilitates individual and profit accountability and inevitably represents a significant portion of most banks' international organisational structure because of the indivisibility of the functions involved.

A geographic structure, on the other hand, focuses on a specific regional orientation, such as the Far East, Americas, Europe, and so forth. By organising part or all of its international function along geographic lines, a bank assumes that the commonality of business conditions in a given region and its own expertise in these areas is of more organisational relevance than the products offered or customer requirements in the particular geographic region. This territorial orientation is perhaps the most traditional form of organisation among international banks in that it reflects the prototype international function which was built around foreign correspondent bank relationships and the financing of short term trade flows. At a minimum, all banks offer at least a portion of their international services under a geographic designation.

Finally, perhaps the newest structural orientation is based on the customer itself, in the form of industry or sectoral groupings around which part or all of the international function is organised. As international banks have come to grips with the greater sophistication of their non-bank customers and their requirements, an increasing number have begun to orient their structure towards servicing what are perceived as the particular needs of individual industry groups. What began, for example, as a specialist staff function providing technical services for lending officers working with the oil or shipping industries, became a line function with responsibility for the energy or transportation sectors. The next step was to create similar line responsibility for all other customers—governmental, chemical, forest products and the rest—on a sectoral basis.

In practice, this customer orientation is effectively a combination of the product/functional and territorial form of organisation using the customer as the focal point. It can also be argued that this third format is nothing more than a particular combination of the original two in that there is a unique balance between territorial and product considerations with the customer representing the focal point of that balance. Consequently, this can be regarded as a swing towards functionalism, in that geographic expertise in the form of the international department simply becomes another function along with, say, investment banking activities, rather than a self-standing bank within a bank.

TYPICAL ORGANISATIONAL STRUCTURES

In practice, every international function is organised with varying elements of several of these three structures. What differs is the relative degree of emphasis on each in the organisational chart as well as such factors as the influence of particular individuals in the organisation, the physical size of the bank, the traditional characteristics of a given bank's business and the willingness to make major organisational changes to maximise profits or provide better customer services. The most prevalent and traditional structure is one based on territorial or geographic lines with certain separate functional groups reporting to the same senior officer. Thus most of the bank's customer-oriented lending and service activities would be grouped as in Figure 5.1 on a regional basis, with internally-oriented functions such as money dealing and staff services organised functionally. There is, therefore, a clear differentiation between the domestic and international functions of the bank at the operating and customer level, while within the international functions individual territories would exist relatively independently of each other. The structure shown in Figure 5.1 is typical of most American banks. Obviously the larger institutions have a greater degree of complexity and number of functions, but the essential components are generally common to most US banks.

This type of structure, in which the international function not only funds part or all of its requirements, but also makes its own credit decisions clearly creates a 'bank within a bank' orientation and mentality. American and other institutions which are organised along these lines believe that the nature of international business is so distinct from that carried on domestically that the risks of separate development and poor communications are relatively unimportant.

The other traditional structural form is that utilised primarily by Japanese and Continental European banks which have an international department organised along territorial lines but without the extent of functional responsibility prevalent in US institutions. In many respects, such a global organisational form is essentially functional with the international department charged primarily with the function of dealing with overseas banks and financing international trade. Unlike the structures described in Figure 5.1, such key functions as customer lending and treasury/money dealing are centralised on a bank-wide basis outside the international function. Such a relatively functional and centralised organisation is described in Figure 5.2.

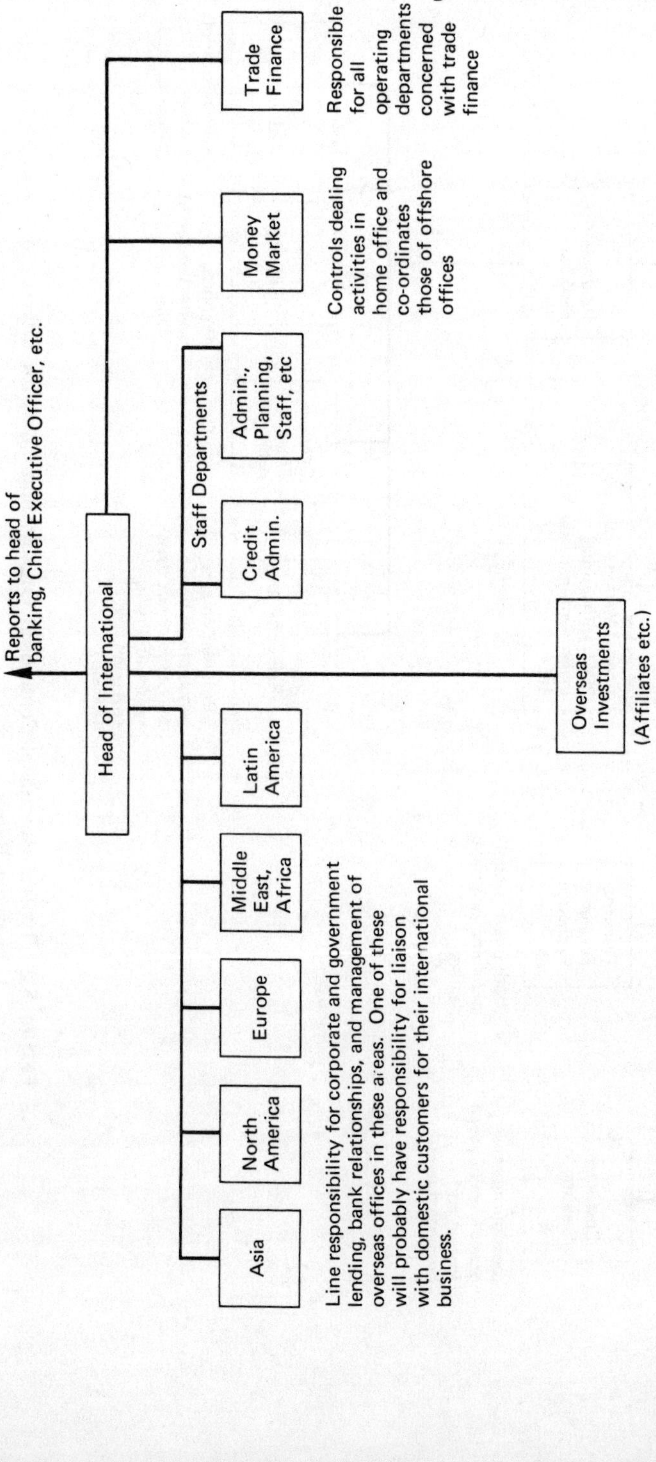

FIGURE 5.1 Typical Territorial/Regional Organisation Chart for International Banks

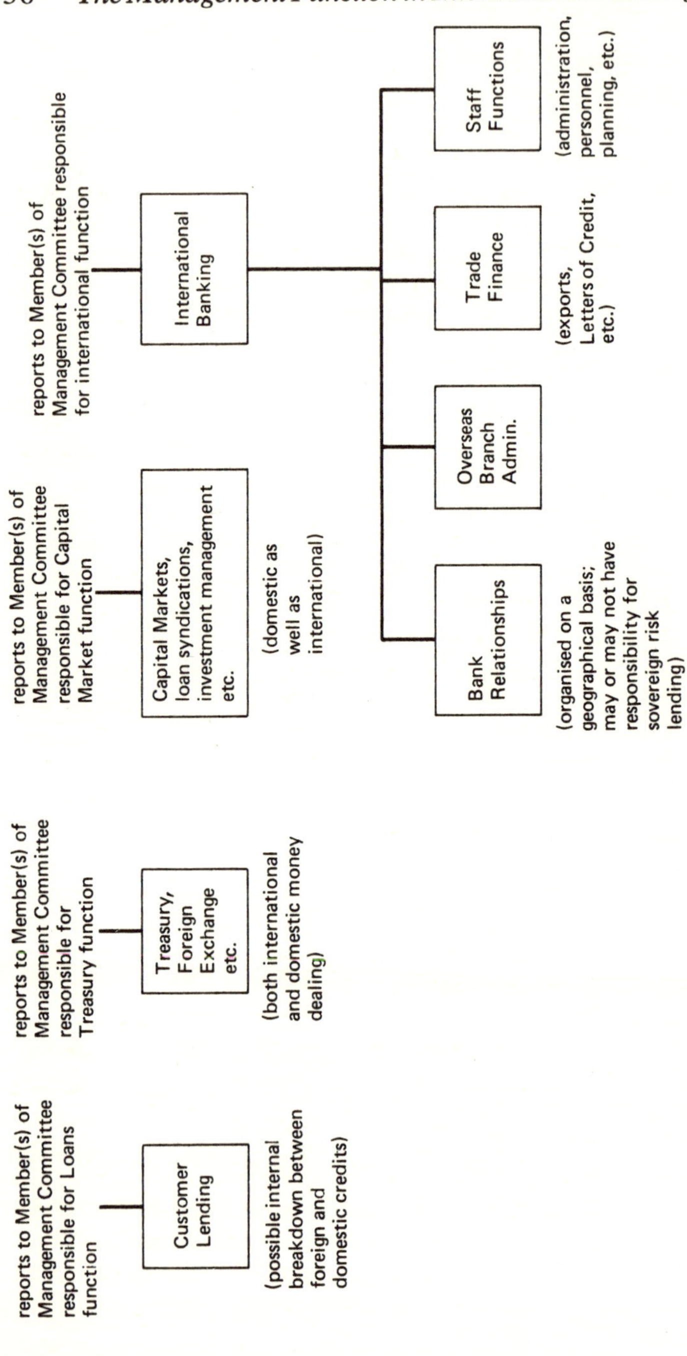

FIGURE 5.2 Typical Functional/Centralised Organisation Chart for International Banks

The Japanese, European and other banks which utilise this type of organisational format thus require a considerable extent of functional interaction when dealing with an international corporate customer's loan request, an overseas branch money market problem, a participation in a syndicated credit or similar transaction. Most of the bank's sophisticated credit skills tend to be centralised in the customer lending function which may or may not also have responsibility for vetting sovereign risk exposure, so that its views on a lending transaction involving an international department customer must be solicited. The same type of dotted line or functional relationship may be involved when an overseas branch responsible to the international banking function takes a mismatch or foreign exchange position, or when a branch manager is offered a participation in a syndicated loan to a customer in his own market area.

Efforts to create an optimum balance between a functional/product and geographic orientation have led to what is known as the matrix organisation, developed by several leading American institutions, whereby functional and geographic specialisation are each given deliberate emphasis on a bank-wide basis, to ensure appropriate communications within the bank and to improve customer service by bringing to bear a totality of different specialist functions. Under such a scheme as carried to its logical extreme, for example, every customer of the bank falls into a certain industry or sectoral category and is serviced on a line basis by a specialist in that category. At the same time, a geographic and/or product-oriented group of specialists interacts with the customer specialists to provide staff support. By assigning primary customer responsibility to an industry specialist, such banks tend to break down or even eliminate the historic distinction between domestic and international in their efforts to adapt to the perceived requirements of the multinational corporations. Primary customer responsibility can also be given to a geographic specialist with a knowledge of that customer's base of operations; in turn, he is able to call on a wide range of specialist knowledge throughout the bank to service his customers' needs. In its ideal form, a customer would have at his service perhaps three types of specialist bankers —one who was intimately familiar with his sector and had overall responsibility, another who offered individual products such as money management services, and a third who had a detailed knowledge of the geographic areas of interest to the client.

More typically, individual bank organisations in practice tend to fall between the simplified, archetypal organisational forms described above. Rather than adopt a pure matrix or functional approach, many banks utilise a variant by which certain customers or types of customers are serviced by line officers outside the traditional domestic–international organisational structure without actually eliminating that particular distinction. A specific customer group—say energy-related customers or large multinational firms—would be split out from the straightforward domestic–international organisation and covered on a line or staff basis by specialists in that group. Quite often such a compromise variant represents a transition towards the full matrix structure from the traditional geographic orientation.

The comprehensive international functions of US and UK banks which group all possible internationally-oriented activities are, in effect, the ultimate territorial organisation. On the other hand, the Continental European or Japanese structure is strongly product-oriented in the sense that international is viewed as a specific product or function along with corporate lending, capital markets and money market activities which are carried on with little territorial distinction.

FACTORS INFLUENCING ORGANISATIONAL STRUCTURE

In practice, the actual choice of organisational emphasis reflects the physical size of a given bank, the influence and background of key individuals in senior management, the bank's historical development in the international market, and the nature of its domestic and international business.

Size is a key determinant of organisation, not only because of the physical resources which a larger bank can bring to bear, but also because of the problems of such an organisation in responding efficiently and effectively to the needs of customers as well as staff. For a far-flung, world-wide organisation offering hundreds of services to thousands of customers from dozens of branches and offices throughout the world, movement towards a matrix-type organisation may be a necessary step to avoid either administrative chaos or the inability to bring to bear the specific expertise needed by a particular customer. By the same token, only the larger organisations can afford the expense of highly paid staffs of customer, product and geographic specialists.

The human factor is also an essential determinant of organisational structure. An individual or individuals who have built a large and profitable international function over a period of decades are unlikely, in the absence of significant outside pressures, to completely remodel the structure which they fashioned and which has become the basis of their influence in the bank.

On the other hand, the arrival of a new chief executive or head of international—particularly one from outside the organisation—or a reorganisation within the international function, may well offer the opportunity to change a structure to meet the requirements of the new management and/or the needs of the marketplace. The background of the leadership of an international function is also important. A traditional international banker oriented towards relationships with other bankers is naturally inclined towards a structure with a primarily geographic basis, while a newcomer with experience outside the banking industry may be more prone to orient international functions along customer or product lines.

Finally, the nature and historic evolution of a bank's traditional business is also a major determinant of a particular organisational structure. A bank with historical ties to, or a major branch network in a given region is unlikely to give up entirely its geographic orientation, while a relative newcomer to the international scene may be more inclined to specialise in particular customer groups or services which are seen to be attractive at the present time. Such a newcomer might even wish to dispense with the traditional global orientation, which subsumes activity throughout the world and the necessity of a desk officer for each country in the world, in favour of a more pragmatic, targeted approach oriented towards high potential areas and functions. By the same token, a bank with its domestic origins in a particular speciality—say a US regional bank with a petroleum industry orientation or a Swiss bank with an investment management tradition—will probably choose an international structure which reflects this dominant domestic emphasis. Such a traditional functional commitment often requires a global management orientation as opposed to what can be regarded as an artificial distinction between domestic and international operations.

Given the evolution of external forces and the response to them of individual banks, it is hardly surprising that many organisational structures are in a period of flux or transition and that banks' senior managements are often dissatisfied with the performance of current structures. In the first place, particularly among larger banks, there are serious problems of reconciling, on the one hand, size and complexity of structure with, on the other hand, flexibility and responsiveness to needs of staff and customers. While a matrix-type organisation for a large bank can be intellectually satisfying on paper, in practice the necessary interaction and communication among a number of individuals from different parts of the organisation, each of which has some kind of responsibility for the relationship, can lead to significant delays in the decision-making process, frustration on the part of bank officers who feel they spend more time relating to other officers in the bank than in actually doing the business which interests them, and in the end the lack of responsive and constructive customer services for which the organisation was designed. On the other hand, smaller banks, or those without the array of specialist talents and products, find it increasingly difficult to compete for the business of customers who have substantial and sophisticated requirements with a global orientation.

Secondly, organisational structures are invariably hampered by a shortage of key personnel who possess the appropriate ingredients of management skills, credit judgement, business development talent and specialist expertise. Such an increasing gap between supply and demand for human resources is understandable in an industry which has grown enormously in physical size as well as number of participants. The opening up of a new offshore financial centre, for example, not only increases demand for more branch managers, more staff support in home office and more systems to handle the increased volume of business, but also brings to the scene entirely new institutions formed to exploit that particular market. Placing the title of branch manager or private placement specialist after the name of an individual does not necessarily endow him with the requisite talents, and organisational structures must often be modified to reflect such weaknesses.

SPECIFIC ORGANISATIONAL RESPONSES

When asked to characterise their existing organisational structure in these terms, 31, or over 80 per cent of the 37 banks responding considered their structures to be primarily geographic in orientation. The remaining one-sixth of the total, which includes primarily larger US banks, regarded their approach as more functionally or matrix-oriented with a balance between geographical and functional specialisation. Another one-sixth of the total, which presently considers itself primarily geographic in focus, is moving towards a more functional orientation.

The matrix or balanced functional/geographic orientation is principally an American phenomenon, but several of the non-American banks are moving in this direction. Those banks which are most enthusiastic about matrix management tend to be the largest institutions which have a real problem in what one banker called 'the management of size'. With a matrix structure, primary customer responsibility can be given either to a product specialist—say the bank's chemicals expert for a foreign chemical company—or the geographic specialist—say the branch manager in the country in which that particular chemical company is located. Thus in any given matrix organisation one orientation—geographic, functional or customer—must dominate to a certain extent to produce effective results.

Most banks, however, consider that such a matrix system is too complex, disruptive for customer relationships and expensive for their particular organisation to implement. To achieve the desired result of improved internal co-ordination and customer service, other approaches are preferred. One is to select a specific group of customers whose business will be handled outside the traditional territorial organisation; another is to have both the international and domestic departments report to the same senior officer who can, therefore, ensure that appropriate co-ordination takes place. A final approach is to designate an individual or group within the domestic or international function which has co-ordinating responsibility for assisting an account officer in another function.

In addition to improving co-ordination and maximising the level and breadth of expertise applied to a customer's problems, movement towards a functional orientation is justified by many bankers because it enables them to develop and market new and existing products and services, which might not otherwise be the case in a purely geographical structure. As such areas of specialist expertise are developed in the bank's effort to differentiate its product line, they are established as functional units with specific profit responsibility reporting to a senior international officer. For the same reasons, existing specialist services may be taken out of a territorial organisation and given separate reporting channels to the head of international.

In terms of relationship with the domestic functions of their bank, roughly one-quarter of the 40 institutions interviewed have some form of customer line responsibility which cuts across the domestic–international distinction. Of the nine banks which have such a structure, six are North American. Most banks confirmed that the decision to modify their traditional structure was a highly political one, involving the areas of responsibility of key management officers, and that the question of appropriate structures was reviewed frequently. It is interesting to note that the presence of a matrix organisation does not necessarily imply the existence of a multinational or other group which cuts across traditional geographic lines; several banks have established bank-wide functional responsibilities without modifying the basic geographic breakdown between domestic and international customers. Banks which are relatively new to corporate lending both domestically and internationally find co-ordination problems relatively simple to resolve, while those which have substantial and long standing corporate lending business tend to be reluctant to reshuffle customer account responsibilities.

One of the dominant impressions gained from conversations with senior bankers is the absence of total satisfaction with any given organisational structure and the constant search for an appropriate blend of geographic, functional and customer orientation. The problem of reconciling a large and complex organisation with such factors as customer objectives, profit accountability and staff job satisfaction is a considerable one, which is complicated by considerations of personalities and the entrenched positions of key individuals in a given organisation.

FUNCTIONING OF THE ORGANISATION

The actual functioning of a given organisation in terms of decision-making structure is the second focus of this chapter. The vital decisions in international banking relate to credit, staffing, pricing, product, marketing, network, asset and liability structure and other factors, but given the nature and tradition of banking the credit decision-making process tends to assume a position of prominence. Quite apart from the obvious importance of credit quality to a bank's performance, most banks are managed by professional bankers who have risen in the organisation through an extended period of exposure to the lending process, and may be unlikely to voluntarily disassociate themselves from the process, whatever their level of responsibility.

In differentiating the various approaches to decision-making in international banks, two distinctions can be made. Firstly, banks differ in the extent of centralisation of decision-making with particular reference to the credit process. Secondly, they can also be characterised by the degree of diffusion of the decision-making process among individuals at various levels of the organisation.

THE ISSUE OF CENTRALISATION

The extent of centralisation of the process is reflected in both formal and informal organisational charts. At one extreme is the highly centralised organisation where most credit and other decisions are made by one or more individuals in home office with officers in the field used primarily to develop proposals and implement home office decisions. At the other extreme is a decentralised organisation where most business decisions are delegated to officers in the field with direct customer and market contact while home office functions primarily to determine strategy and policy, provide staff services and operating guidelines to regional or local operations and solve problems as they arise.

The choice of degree of centralisation is usually determined by the factors of size and complexity of structure, the background and orientation of senior bank and international management, the nature of the bank's business and the availability of qualified and trusted personnel. A very large bank with a highly complex organisational structure may find it virtually impossible to function competitively without delegating most credit and other decisions to individuals or committees who can provide a timely and constructive response to a customer. On the other hand, equally large banks with more traditional and simplified forms of territorial or product structure can funnel virtually all significant business decisions to a core of senior headquarters personnel which provides a more or less efficient response to officers in the field. In the former category are principally the larger US banks with a complex, matrix-type organisational structure, while in the more centralised category are the great majority of European, Canadian and Japanese banks which traditionally have made credit and other decisions centrally. While size thus does not necessarily determine degree of centralisation, complexity of structure does play a significant role.

The background and orientation of senior management is also important in that a tradition of decades of centralised decision-making in a given institution is extremely difficult to modify. Such a tradition may reflect the lack of familiarity or 'comfort' of senior management with international business, past problems which have placed an indelible imprint on organisational behaviour, or simply the combination of habit and self-interest which perpetuates management practices over an extended period of time. Once again, a radical change in management personalities or outside circumstances may force an equivalent modification of the degree of centralisation.

The nature of a bank's business influences centralisation in several ways. A bank with a large amount of retail or locally-oriented business in foreign countries is likely to have a significant degree of decentralised decision-making, while one with a limited number of large, wholesale loan decisions or with a central core of specialist knowledge in, say, the energy sector is more likely to bring decisions back to home office. The availability and personal objectives of qualified staff are also vital considerations. The traditional justification for centralisation of decision-making is the relative absence of such human skills and the consequent need to concentrate credit and other decisions in home office where the experienced individuals are likely to be located. On the other hand, several American banks have made the opposite argument in recent years by placing their limited supply of experienced staff in the field, in regional headquarters, where they can make more responsive, market-related judgements. Of growing force in recent years has been the frustration of overseas or market-oriented officers in centralised organisations where the individual acquires management or customer-related skills in a foreign environment but is not permitted, in his view, sufficient decision-making authority to match these skills. This problem is compounded by the physical difficulty of communicating to the decision-makers in a far-off home or regional office the background to, and reasons for, a particular credit or other decision which he is proposing.

Such a possible conflict between the field and home office is inevitable in any international organisation, but the problem is particularly acute in international banking because of the importance of the credit decision-making process and the relative lack of experience of so many international bankers in this rapidly developing market. A particular characteristic of recent years among some US banks, therefore, has been the increasing degree of decentralisation as the banks mature internationally and overseas-based staff return to more senior management positions in home office, where they are in a position to correct what they regarded as an overcentralised structure when overseas.

It is interesting to note that length and extent of experience internationally is not a major factor in determining the extent of centralisation. Some of the most experienced international institutions are the most centralised, while some relative newcomers have made the boldest decentralisation moves.

Management Response to Centralisation

Of the 40 banks interviewed in the sample, only 13, or one-third regard their decision-making process as essentially decentralised, with the balance basically centralised in nature. Roughly the same ratio of centralised versus decentralised structures were shown by the North American sub-sample and the other institutions. A number of relatively centralised banks expressed the desire to delegate more authority but have been restrained by factors such as the traditional decision-making process within the bank, a perceived shortage of experienced bankers in the field, and the record of past mistakes stemming from delegation of authority. The relative predominance of centralised decision-making indicated by the above sample may actually be understated in the sense that several bankers described themselves as decentralised by virtue of the existence of relatively low credit authorities of, say, $500,000 delegated to the field but admitted that most credit and other decisions were made at home office.

Some of the large American banks take pride in the ability of key officers overseas to make substantial commitments, often up to the bank's legal lending limit, without reference to home office. Other large banks which make such decisions centrally pointed out that their 'turnaround time', or response time, for a credit proposal was rapid enough to offset this apparent disadvantage. Among the smaller banks and those with little international experience, it is accepted that a limited number of very senior officers in home office, often including the bank's chief executive officer, will make all substantive credit, personnel, lending policy and other decisions.

The presence or absence of an overseas regional headquarters does not necessarily imply a corresponding delegation of authority except in purely administrative or staff functions. Many European and Japanese banks which have a domestic retail banking tradition and a collegiate form of management decision-making are quite reluctant to delegate authority, even within home office for wholesale lending decisions, which represent for them not only a considerable commitment, but also a radical change in their collective decision-making process.

Whatever the degree of centralisation, the decision-making process usually involves several levels of management. The typical procedure is to delegate at least a minimum of credit and non-credit authority to branch managers or other senior overseas officers—perhaps authority to commit from $500,000 to $5 million equivalent to a given customer depending on the size of the bank and its degree of centralisation. Commitments above this amount would go to a higher authority in the international function in a regional headquarters or in home office, while in many cases a third tier of authority outside the international function—perhaps including the chief executive or chief credit officer—might be required. Outside the realm of credit, decision-making tends to be even more centralised as decisions involving personnel, compensation, lending policy, asset and liability management and other issues tend to involve enough elements in the organisation, or represent a sufficiently important policy decision, to require some form of central approval.

In all this procedure, informal processes are as important as those laid out in the organisational chart. For example, an officer overseas may have a formal delegation to commit to a particular decision, but if he senses that such a decision might not be well received by a higher authority he may not make it without some informal checkings within the organisation. On the other hand, without a formal delegation, individual officers in market-related positions often make what are in effect commitments to customers and others and are able, by virtue of their personality, track record or personal influence with senior management, to implement those commitments. The presence of a formal decision-making process thus may or may not involve a significant review of the particular decision in view of the importance of the confidence factor; proposals of a trusted subordinate may be waved through while those of a less experienced individual or one who does not have his superior's total confidence will be critically reviewed.

The importance of the informal management processes is brought out by a question in the 40-bank survey which asked whether a written organisation chart existed for the international function. While it is dangerous to read too much into the specific responses, it is interesting that over one-third of the total sample did not have available such a chart. Perhaps more remarkable is the fact that almost one-half of the US and Canadian banks, which are known for their focus on individual responsibility and authority, fell into this category. Reasons given for the lack of a readily available organisation chart included the fact that it was in the process of being revised and that it did not reflect the true allocation of responsibilities. At a minimum, these responses confirm the importance of informal relationships in the typical bank decision-making structure.

THE ISSUE OF DIFFUSION OF AUTHORITY AND RESPONSIBILITY

The other distinguishing feature of a decision-making process is the diffusion of authority and responsibility among individuals in the organisational structure. Such diffusion may be measured by the number of individuals involved in a given decision and is characterised by the distinction between individual and group, or committee, responsibility. At one extreme is the typical American bank structure where one senior individual has responsibility for the entire international function and reports to a single member of the senior management of the bank. The head of international in turn delegates specific responsibility for individual products and territories to individuals who each have a clearly defined profit responsibility together with individual decision-making authority. Such a function is relatively formal, structured and compartmentalised, with emphasis on definition of individual responsibility and authority.

At the other extreme is the highly diffuse Continental European or Japanese approach where several senior individuals, usually members of a senior management committee which effectively manages the bank, have responsibility for individual aspects of the bank's international business. While an international department exists, this usually encompasses primarily the traditional bank-to-bank and trade-financing business on a territorial basis. Other key functions such as corporate lending, capital market activities and money dealing are the ultimate responsibility of one or more members of the senior management committee, who ordinarily cover both the domestic and international aspects of that particular function. Such a senior management group meets frequently to make most significant—and sometimes minor—credit and other decisions. While a junior credit committee of international personnel may also exist, it is this senior management committee sitting in effect as a credit committee which ultimately makes most credit decisions. Japanese and Continental European banks thus tend to have a collective, flexible and interactive management approach without the emphasis on individual responsibility and authority prevalent among US institutions. In some cases, one notes a trend away from shared responsibility in the former type of organisation towards increasing specialisation; the international function, for one, may be assigned to one or more members of the senior management committee as it becomes a larger and more complex aspect of the business.

Diffusion of specific responsibility for credit decisions can exist in any structure through the use of a credit committee, which represents the standard process for most international banks. Those with single international heads as well as senior committee management usually make use of a group decision-making process at various levels for credit approvals. The size, composition and influence of such a committee depends upon the influence of individual personalities as well as the objectives of the committee. One or more individuals such as the chief executive, the head of the credit function or a senior international officer may dominate the committee and its proceedings. In addition to actually making credit decisions, the committee may serve also as an educational and communications forum for individuals not directly involved in the credit process. A variety of titles—Credit Allocation, Loan/Credit Policy, Asset/Liability Management, etc.—is used for what can range from simply rubber stamping a past credit approval to making broad policy decisions covering pricing, lending policy, personnel, network management and other factors.

The use of a relatively diffuse process reflects a variety of factors, including a perceived lack of qualifications of individual banking officers, historical decision-making tradition on a group basis, and a natural tendency among bankers to become and remain part of the essential credit decision-making process. In countries such as Japan where business decisions are traditionally made from the bottom up on a collective basis, such a process is quite natural. In Continental European banks which have always been run by a management committee on a collegiate basis and where senior management may not yet be comfortable with international exposure, the same is true. On the other hand, in American institutions where individual effort and accountability are features of business life, diffusion of the decision-making process is more limited and takes the form primarily of a credit review committee, which often only ratifies decisions already taken in practice, or exists primarily for communication or educational purposes.

A relatively diffuse decision-making structure has the obvious advantage of bringing to bear the combined wisdom of a large number of interested and experienced individuals, as well as communicating policy and practice to a wide range of officers. On the other hand, by its nature it may significantly hamper individual initiative and accountability, in particular as the natural tendency of any group decision is to impose terms and conditions important to individuals in the group but possibly of little value in the real competitive world. The committee process is particularly difficult in international banking where not only may several committee members have little international experience, but also where propositions must often be supported by an individual who has ultimate responsibility but who cannot be physically present to defend his proposal.

In countries such as the US and UK with a single tier Board of Directors, such a body is rarely involved in day-to-day lending or other decisions, but rather functions in a review or audit capacity and in the approval of strategic decisions such as acquisitions or major expansion moves. The same is generally true of the top Board (Aufsichtsrat, Conseil d'Administration, etc.) of Continental European and Japanese banks which also have a second or operating Board (Vorstand, Direction Générale, Board of General Managers, Board of Managing Directors, etc.). It is the latter, however, which plays the dominant role in the more diffuse and flexible decision-making structure in such countries. The role of the chief executive officer in the day-to-day decision-making process varies considerably throughout the world, with little correlation as to country. Some chief executives continue to involve themselves in day-to-day customer-related and other decisions, while others have restricted themselves to a policy-making role.

An effort was made to quantify the extent to which banks in the questionnaire sample had a single head of international with responsibility for all international business including credit decision-making authority and Euro-currency money market operations. Of the 40 banks, 29 or roughly three-quarters described their structure in such terms, while in the remaining quarter several different members of senior management were responsible for various aspects of overseas business. In reality, however, the latter number is probably understated as many banks with supposedly one head of international have centralised either corporate credit authority or the global treasury function outside the area of responsibility of this individual. With very few exceptions, however, the 21 US and Canadian banks interviewed did centralise all these aspects of their international activities under one individual. Of the non-North American banks, therefore, somewhat over one-half claimed to have a single head of all international operations.

In the instances where a true single head of the international function exists, he tends to report to a single member of senior management who is either the head of banking (or corporate banking), the chief executive of the bank, or another member of top management. Of the 29 instances in the sample of a single international head, in ten cases he reported directly to the chief executive officer of the bank, in eight instances to the head of banking or corporate banking, and in three cases to an executive management committee.

THE ISSUE OF MANAGEMENT DEVELOPMENT

One of the most important management processes in international banking is the need to recruit, train, compensate, motivate and promote individuals who are capable of meeting the external and internal challenges described earlier in this book. As mentioned previously, in its relatively passive initial phase, fairly simple skills were required in an international function: an understanding of trade finance procedures and risks, an ability to work successfully with other financial institutions, a generalist knowledge of international conditions, and practical skills in money dealing or foreign exchange. Such individuals were not necessarily those best equipped to deal with sophisticated risks, advise corporate customers on financing alternatives or manage a vast world-wide bureaucracy.

In the American banks which took the lead in the post-war development of the international banking sector, it became evident early on that a variety of measures needed to be taken to develop the necessary management, credit, marketing and other skills. The first logical step was to transfer individuals with such skills from domestic banking functions with the objective both of improving the skills level internationally and of increasing the level of mutual understanding between the two functions. There were obvious limitations to such transfers, however, as the individuals being sought after were often those most highly prized by their present department head, while the challenge of international banking did not necessarily appeal to all of them.

The next steps taken by many US institutions were the upgrading of their direct recruitment efforts and the willingness to hire staff from other banks. Institutions which had recruited a variety of individual applicants for a bank-wide training programme now began to seek out and hire more high-potential individuals from business and other graduate schools and place them in a training environment which was at least partially geared for international requirements. Banks which had had a traditional aversion to hiring outsiders or individuals from other banks realised that such recruitment efforts were the only practical means of achieving their ambitious international growth targets. Quite naturally, recruitment efforts centred on individuals from banks with more international sophistication. In fact, many smaller banks find that they do not have the resources available to train the staff they need which must, therefore, be brought in from outside. Within individual banks the skills of existing staff were upgraded by the greater use of training programmes in friendly banks abroad, internal courses in subjects such as credit and marketing often taught by outside specialists, and exposure of selected individuals to outside programmes in advanced management and other techniques.

Along with more selective recruitment and training has come a generally higher level of compensation which is also geared to performance. US bank salaries have been increased considerably to attract high-performance individuals who might otherwise have been attracted to other financial institutions, while starting salaries paid to new recruits and those hired from outside at competitive rates inevitably caused problems with existing salary structures. Such damage was increased with the hiring of specialists who commanded salaries quite out of tune with commercial banking scales.

While US institutions have thus made strenuous efforts to develop the skills of their staff at all levels, other banks, particularly in Continental Europe, have moved more slowly. In many European countries, the annual intake of new employees is selected without particular regard to level of academic achievement or particular skills, and training programmes are geared to educating such a broad range of individuals in the traditional fundamentals of banking. Only when the individual has succeeded in passing the required bank-wide standard tests may he be considered for an international assignment, from which point on he is expected to climb the ladder of promotion as did his international predecessors for the past few decades. In such countries it is still regarded as undesirable to hire an experienced outsider, and executive mobility has been only a fraction of that in the US. As their international ambitions increase, however, such banks are finding themselves obliged to recruit a more select group of trainees and to hire experienced outsiders, in view of the limitations on their ability to upgrade existing staff and transfer domestic bankers to the international function.

A number of questions were asked in the 40-bank interview sample to determine the extent to which such changes in the personnel development process had taken place and to analyse in this context the background of the leadership of the bank and the head of international. It is interesting to note, for example, that despite the presumption on the part of many observers that US banks promote younger individuals, there was no significant differentiation in the age at which the present head of international took over his function between, on the one hand, US/Canadian institutions and, on the other, non-North American banks. The average age of the present head of international in a North American bank was 45 when he assumed his job, as opposed to 44 for the other institutions. There would also seem to be no significant difference in mobility at this particular level; in roughly 20 per cent of both the US/Canadian and non-North American samples, the present head of international had been brought in from outside the bank to head this function.

No significant statistical differential between North American and other banks is revealed by another measurement—the holding of a university degree by the present head of international. Roughly two-thirds of the individuals in both subsamples hold such a degree. Finally, some doubt is thrown on the presumption that American banks have moved abroad more aggressively because of the influence of a chief executive who has moved through the international function at some point in his career. Approximately one half of the chief executives of the sample banks have such experience, but the proportion in non-North American banks is 60 per cent compared to 40 per cent for the US and Canadian institutions.

One measure of the effort being made to accelerate the training of high potential staff is the presence or absence of a training programme within the international function which is geared towards university graduates. The existence of such a programme not only brings to light the priority placed on such individuals but also the recognition that the requirements for success in an international banking function may differ from those elsewhere in the bank. Of the 37 banks which responded to this particular question, approximately one-half have such a programme, but the proportion of the US/Canadian sample is 60 per cent as opposed to roughly one-third of the other banks.

From the above it would appear difficult to draw many conclusions about the different behaviour of banks on the basis of nationality—either in terms of level of interest in international business on the part of the chief executive, the relative youth of senior management or its level of education. It would appear, however, that US banks place a greater emphasis on hiring and accelerating the development of high-potential individuals as well as being more willing to hire experienced individuals from other banks. Quite understandably, non-North American banks face greater difficulty in management development, not only because of the problems of overcoming traditional practices, but also because of such very material factors as the need for a banker to be fluent in English, which is the language of international banking, as well as familiar with the Euro-currency banking practices which have been developed from the American model. A particular problem for American and other banks alike is the difficulty in locating individuals, particularly of other nationalities, who are sufficiently mobile to be willing to move from assignment to assignment in a prearranged career path.

A common problem faced by all banks has been to motivate and promote high-potential individuals in organisational structures often characterised by promotion through seniority, entrenched positions held by key individuals with considerable power in the organisation, and compensation policies geared towards simpler and less demanding responsibilities. The senior managements of many banks have found it most difficult to open up such organisations to both insiders and outsiders who have management and other skills needed to succeed in the current international environment, with the result that many organisation charts reflect an unhappy compromise between traditional approaches and more market, product or performance-oriented individuals.

Even where the difficult decisions have been taken to restructure organisations, there remains the problem of motivating high-performance individuals in an increasingly large and structured organisation, where the relationship between personal effort and results often seems tenuous to the individual involved. In such cases a blend of incentive compensation and improved accountability for given functions, customers or geographical areas is often utilised to provide the appropriate level of job satisfaction.

THE GROWING IMPORTANCE OF STAFF FUNCTIONS

The rapid growth and increasing complexity of international banking have generated a significant need for new and sophisticated staff departments to assist the senior management of an international function. Data processing techniques must be developed and refined, not only to process vastly increased volumes of transactions, but also to provide management with vital information to run the business. The problems of recruiting, training, compensating and developing career paths for staff in a growing and increasingly sophisticated international bank must be resolved by a human resources function that is more than the senior clerical job it may once have been. Tax, premises, legal, economics, marketing and other staff departments may have to be developed from scratch.

One of the most important grouping of staff functions, however, is that of planning and control, which exists to assist senior management in setting objectives and strategy and devising the systems which implement these decisions and monitor performance. In an ideal world, this integrated process involves long-term planning with regular updating of detailed objectives and a carefully articulated strategy, as well as thc generation of sufficient data to evaluate performance and permit corrective action to be taken on a timely basis.

In practice, however, international banks face a number of problems in achieving this ideal. While most banks prepare a short and possibly medium-term financial plan, quite often this reflects little more than an exercise in statistics designed to show appropriate growth and development from one year to the next. Truly integrated strategic planning involving such factors as long-term product, staff and network planning is relatively rare for a variety of reasons. Quite apart from the relative inexperience of many senior bankers in the more sophisticated management techniques, there is a frequent tendency to deprecate planning in view of the presence of major exogenous or uncontrollable variables, the need for sometimes arbitrary allocation of costs and revenues, and the presumption that profit planning implies undue assumption of risk in such sectors as foreign exchange and deposit dealing. The more precise definition of departmental profits might well undermine a given individual's claim to status in the international function. Over time, however, more banks have come to recognise that planning is a management tool designed to establish a rational basis for achieving objectives, rather than a collection of numbers which will be used as an arbitrary stick to beat those who do not achieve them. Exogenous variables such as interest and exchange rates can be isolated by specialists so as to define more precisely the controllable factors on which management should be evaluated. While arbitrary distinctions such as allocation of costs and revenues or determination of the pool rate of funds are often necessary, their weaknesses are more than offset by the need of management to determine the approximate relative profitability of given functions and sectors of operation.

In an increasingly complex and sophisticated environment, the role of these staff functions has often increased to the point where they come into conflict with the revenue generating departments of the international function. Conflicts between lending operations on the one hand, and the tax or legal departments on the other, may become highly complex and involve a number of ramifications. The net result is to place even more importance on the management function in an international bank which must weigh the various conflicting considerations and make an intelligent decision. The head of international has thus become increasingly dependent upon his staff specialists to whom he must necessarily delegate a significant amount of authority, just as he has often been obliged by the pressure of other responsibilities to step away from line decisions in areas such as the lending function. To an increasing extent, therefore, he must intervene to sort out problems involving the conflicting points of view of two or more staff and line officers.

6 Marketing and Business Development

The management practice of marketing, which can be defined as the identification of a target clientele, the development of specific products, and their pricing and distribution to the selected range of customers, is a relative newcomer to the field of banking in general and international banking in particular. In their traditional mode as described in Chapter 4, bankers considered themselves as purveyors of services required by customers and lenders of short-term funds to finance trade, at the request of such customers, on a virtually risk-free basis. Other international banks were collaborators and sources of useful business.

By the mid-1970s, however, most international bankers had come to realise that they had to compete to achieve their profit and other goals, and that competition in the financial markets meant dealing with the elements of marketing: determining who the customer was, what the customer wanted, developing products and services to meet this demand, pricing these services to meet the competition and provide for a satisfactory return, and developing the appropriate channels through which they were to be sold. While marketing as a concept is now more acceptable to bankers, there is still a residual view that marketing is both unbankerly, in that it is not correct or professional to sell one's services, and unnecessary, in the sense that traditional relationships and quality of product are sufficient to do the job. Many banks have created internal marketing functions or hired outside marketing experts in an effort to come to grips with the problem, but by and large marketing concepts as practiced in industry have not significantly penetrated the thinking of senior bankers. On balance, however, the impact of competition and the increased sophistication of corporate customers have obliged banks to think more seriously about product development and product differentiation.

SURVEY OF 30 SENIOR CORPORATE FINANCIAL OFFICERS

Before going into the detail of the marketing strategy and tactics of international banks, it might be appropriate to review the results of a customer survey conducted by the author in mid-1978. This survey of 30 senior financial officers of major multinational firms was undertaken to provide an appropriate context for the discussion of international banks' marketing and business development strategy. The firms which completed the questionnaire attached as Appendix C are located in the US, UK, Continental Europe and Asia and represent a small but reasonably representative sample of the heavily-solicited multinational corporations which are the declared target of most international banks' marketing efforts.

The questions in the survey focused on the respondents' attitudes towards adding new banks to their list of relationships; their evaluation of existing banking relationships, and what they consider weaknesses in the performance of international banks. While these comments naturally reflect only one side of the banker–customer dialogue, useful conclusions may be drawn from individual comments and some fairly well defined response patterns.

International bankers can anticipate an interested and open, albeit critical, reception when they try to establish an initial relationship with a multinational corporation. Less than 10 per cent of the respondents were unprepared under any circumstances to establish a new banking relationship, while only two of the thirty financial officers actively discouraged initial or 'cold' calls by a bank with whom he did not yet do business. The almost universal attitude is that such newcomers often bring new ideas and approaches to their problems and may represent a useful learning experience, particularly when a company is entering a new market or is dissatisfied with an existing banking relationship. One regional treasurer of a major US multinational firm welcomes the calls of new banks even though his region has existing relationships with 147 different institutions. Such heavily-solicited officers try to select out fringe banking institutions and make it clear to the others how difficult it will be to develop an actual relationship. As a senior treasury officer of a major British multinational puts it: 'we try to strike a balance between containing perpetual growth in our banking relationships, but at the same time neither slam the door rudely in anyone's face nor close our minds to the creative thinking that can sometimes be stimulated by a new contact'.

While they thus feel obliged to receive new prospective bankers, these financial officers are often critical of bankers who have nothing specific to offer—so-called courtesy visits—expect to do business after the first call, or oversell their institution rather than determining what are the corporation's needs. Many financial officers made it clear that prospective bankers can receive a positive welcome only if they have done their homework in advance and are fully competitive in the terms they offer.

When asked to name the criteria used in selecting a new bank relationship, the financial officers cited as the principal factor the offering by a given bank of a new or imaginative solution to a specific problem. Roughly 40 per cent of the respondents cited this factor as their primary consideration, while the ability to accept a specific credit risk ranked as the second most important individual determinant. This emphasis on innovative solutions in a market characterised by little product differentiation places a heavy burden on bankers but it does provide an incentive for the banker to do more than trot out services which are indistinguishable from those of his competitors. The importance of these two criteria taken together also highlights the clients' preference for a one-off specific transaction to initiate a new relationship, rather than an across-the-board approach which might, of course, develop over time.

Recognising that a blend of motives is usually involved in such a decision, another analytical approach is to aggregate the three criteria ranked most highly by individual respondents. The most frequently cited criteria are the two factors already mentioned (imagination and assumption of credit risk) plus the fineness of terms quoted and the speed and responsiveness of the bank's decision-making process, each of which was cited as one of their three top criteria by more than 15, or one-half of the financial officers polled. Other criteria mentioned, in decreasing order of frequency, were the ability of the bank to step up itself for the full amount of a given requirement, personal relationships with the account officer, and flexibility with regard to documentation.

Perhaps the most interesting conclusion to be drawn from the ranking of criteria is the low priority given to the range of services offered by the particular bank, particularly since 'adding to our range of services' is one of the more frequent justifications given by international banks for a particular expansionary move or marketing approach. Fewer than 10 per cent of the respondents thus mentioned size of network and range of services as one of the three most important decision-making criteria. The relative unimportance of this criterion for the larger multinationals can be attributed to their acknowledgement that different banks have different strengths and weaknesses, and that the financial officers prefer to use individual banks for specific one-off purposes which reflect a coincidence of respective skills and requirements—e.g. a willingness to accept a particular risk, or an acknowledged skill in moving money from one place to another. Another criterion which surprisingly did not apparently carry more weight with the corporate financial officers was personal relationship with the account officer; only one-quarter of the respondents mentioned this as one of their three principal criteria. Superficially, this level of priority would appear inconsistent with the standard corporate criticism that account officers are changed too frequently; on balance, one might conclude that today's corporate treasurers tend to make a more impersonal and objective evaluation of their bank's capabilities and accept, however reluctantly, the frequent rotation of account responsibility. Personal chemistry is always an important factor in this type of relationship, but evidently other considerations of a more objective nature tend to be more important.

CRITICISM OF INTERNATIONAL BANKERS

By far the most frequently expressed criticism of the business development approach of international banks to corporate solicitation is the lack of preparation and understanding of the latter's business and requirements. This was cited by almost one-half of the respondents as their major criticism of the initial approach by international banks, and by over half as one of the three principal weaknesses of such an approach. Three other complaints—the lack of a specific service or product to propose, the inability to commit responsively without time-consuming recourse to home office, and uncompetitive terms—were mentioned as one of their three principal criticisms by roughly one-third of the respondents, while inflexibility and over-legalistic thinking with regard to loan documentation was mentioned as a significant problem by a number of other financial officers. Non-American corporations are particularly sensitive to the frequent practice of American banks of not only insisting on lengthy legal documentation, but also permitting their lawyers to dominate documentary negotiations.

It would thus appear that a significant number of international bankers are perceived not to have done their advance homework before approaching a potential client and therefore find themselves selling a rather undifferentiated product, usually loans or deposit services. A typical quotation is the following from a US corporate treasurer: 'I am somewhat indignant when they start off with the desire and expectation of doing business with this office without doing a nominal amount of homework on our organisation from readily available sources.' And the effort must be a sustained one, to quote a regional treasurer for an oil major: 'Those banks who have successfully made the entry have invariably been willing to undertake a great deal of leg work to find the deal that makes the entry—and then to follow it through. Many banks are not willing to put in this effort.' Another common view was voiced by a corporate treasurer who criticised 'representatives who clearly intend to sell the bank and really have no interest in our group'.

While bankers may be quite convinced of the unique advantages of the services they are selling, corporate treasurers confronted by dozens of such presentations may have a different view. The frustration about international banks' decision-making processes reflects the contrast between the enthusiastic reception of a calling officer interested in establishing a new relationship, and the more considered reaction, often many weeks later, of a senior credit committee which brings other considerations to bear on the proposal.

One specific technique used by international banks to establish an initial relationship is price-cutting, and the responses of the 30 financial officers to a patently below-market quote are quite informative. Over half react positively to such attractive offers of finance or pricing methods, but unless the offering bank has a rational justification for its finer rate—such as a particular knowledge of the credit risk or a specific foreign exchange position of its own—it is almost universally seen to be a loss leader which will be recouped at the client's expense at a later date. Raw price cutting without a rational justification is regarded by a minority of the responding sample as a negative reflection on the professionalism of the bank. Corporate treasurers thus often accept such an underpriced offer as a reflection of the competitive state of the market, but recognise, as the treasurer of a leading UK multinational put it, that 'a bank which quotes terms which are so advantageous to us as to be clearly out of line with the market will win the business but probably not achieve its obvious objective'.

When asked to evaluate existing banking relationships, the respondents cited as their dominant consideration once again the bank's understanding of the customer's business and requirements together with the willingness, which usually stems from such an understanding, of the bank to stick with the customer in difficult circumstances. Almost half of the respondents cited such an understanding as the principal desideratum, while the top criterion mentioned by the second largest number of banks, the fineness of terms quoted, was cited by only 4 of the 30 respondents. If one aggregates the three criteria given the highest priority, understanding of the business (21 responses) and fineness of terms (17 responses) are joined by that of speed and responsiveness of decision-making process (also 17 responses); over one-half of all the respondents thus cited these three considerations as being dominant in their evaluation of existing relationships. It goes without saying that a profound understanding of a client's business can lead not only to fine pricing but also to a quick response time. Other factors mentioned frequently were an imaginative response to a specific problem (12 responses) and the ability of a single bank to meet a given requirement from its own resources (11 responses). Over one-third of the financial officers thus preferred a bank able to avoid the delays and complications often associated with the syndication of a given loan. Only four of the financial officers gave range of services as one of their top three criteria—once again because the large multinationals appear to look to individual banks for their particular strengths and would apparently prefer to pick and choose among a variety of banks.

By relating the criteria applied to new and existing relationships, it would appear that financial officers select new banks on their ability to meet a specific need; once the bank has thus established a relationship, it is evaluated on the basis of its understanding and constancy as well as fineness of pricing and speed of response.

While one can discount some of these reactions as reflecting an understandable preoccupation with the client's own objectives rather than an appreciation of the banker's problems, it is reasonable to conclude that a wide range of international bank calling and account officers do not, in fact, bring with them a reasonable understanding of the potential customer's business and a product or service which is perceived as having some utility to that customer. Business development officers would thus appear to be spending an excessive amount of time in selling their own institution or engaging in social conversation rather than focusing on perceived needs and possible solutions. In many cases the calling officer may not have the necessary expertise to provide the solution desired by the financial officer or, much less, maintain his end of a discussion of possible solutions.

BANKERS' APPROACHES TO MARKETING

If one now addresses the first element of marketing—market research into the requirements of potential customers— it would appear that relatively little objective, original research seems to have been done by banks to determine precisely what their international customers need, although a number of customer attitudinal surveys with some international implications have been commissioned in the US by American banks. Unlike most industrialists, many international bankers appear to feel that they are as well equipped as anyone to determine the requirements of their customers, and, therefore, do not need an outsider's check on their own marketing approach.

In a second marketing aspect, that of developing their lines of products, in most cases bankers have found great difficulty in establishing sufficient product differentiation. They are admittedly competing in an industry characterised by a fungible principal product and a marketplace at times approaching the economic theorist's state of pure competition. Rather than increasing product differentiation and development, international banking competition over the past few years has actually reduced it in many respects through the increasing uniformity of pricing Euro-currency loans and of writing Euro-currency loan agreements. Successful new products such as the concept of pricing loans at a floating rate over the cost of funds and the medium-term negotiable floating rate note have, in fact, been introduced into the market, but the bandwagon effect of intense competition in an open market has made it extremely difficult for the innovator to retain any sustained financial benefit.

For the most part, therefore, the product development function of international banks has taken the form of adopting and/or perfecting established speciality products in which they hope to develop a competitive edge, such as clearing services, export finance, services for wealthy individuals, and merchant banking activities such as the syndication of Euro-currency loans and the origination of private placements. Most international bankers admit that new product development is not likely to produce very exciting results, and their efforts are, therefore, devoted to what are essentially established products.

One of these products is expertise—in speciality functional sectors such as oil or shipping; in executing transactions such as foreign exchange or the movement of funds; and in regional knowledge. By implication, promotion of this expertise is another way of expressing a willingness to accept certain risks not generally assumed by banks. In view of the traditional bankerly emphasis on safety and conservatism, bankers are highly reluctant to suggest that they deliberately take any but the safest of risks, much less use risk as a marketing tool. By deliberately acknowledging their substantial foreign exchange and deposit mismatch positions, however, continental European banks implicitly recognise this marketing speciality, while other institutions advertising their special interest in sectors such as energy and shipping, acknowledge willingness to assume a sectoral risk as a marketing tool.

Another product is the actual range of services, both in terms of geographic coverage as well as extent of commercial and investment banking products. It is only natural that the largest banks are competing on the basis of their ability to provide virtually any financial service anywhere in the world. A third product is quality of service in the form of speed and flexibility of response, quality of performance in such areas as movements of funds, and a personalised service for those customers who are prepared to pay for it. The larger banks are also marketing their ability to commit sufficient funds to meet a customer's requirements so as to avoid the problems often associated with loan syndication.

The pricing of banking products, on the other hand, is not generally regarded as a product to be marketed or as a valid selling approach. While many banks have developed highly sophisticated means of pricing loans as well as other customer services, these calculations are used more as a technique to determine minimum acceptable return rather than as a strategic marketing tool to maximise long term profitability. The impact and extent of competition has generally prevented the banks from using loan pricing in such a strategic context, as competition has been the dominant factor in loan pricing in recent years. Other products such as specialised services can be priced on a more strategic basis, but for the bulk of its revenue base the international bank has to regard competition as the dominant pricing factor.

The customer base to which these products are marketed reflects current perceptions of credit quality, traditional relationships and preferences, and the relative demand for banking services. Most international banks have done a significant amount of thinking about their ideal target client, and the overwhelming majority place at the top of their list the large multinational firm, which is regarded as both highly creditworthy and appropriate in the context of the bank's traditional and preferred orientation towards corporate customers with whom a broadly-based relationship can be established.

Governments and governmental institutions, particularly those in developing countries with a perceived credit risk, tend to be less highly sought after, both for this reason and the difficulty of developing such a broad relationship with a public sector entity. In view of the intense competition for the relatively limited banking requirements of these preferred customers, many banks have subsequently focused on the so-called middle market, or smaller private sector firms, which may carry a higher credit risk but offer the possibility of establishing at an early date a relationship which will hopefully grow as the client does. Over time, therefore, a typical bank's target client base has moved from overseas banking correspondents, to its existing domestic customers' overseas operations, to prime multinational and governmental customers, and finally to a broader range of small and medium-sized private and public sector institutions with a perceived credit risk.

The channels through which these products are marketed have evolved significantly in the past decade for many institutions. In line with the traditional approach of using foreign correspondents as a source of business, such institutions originally attempted to market their services through these correspondents. Over time most banks found that their competitors were picking up this corporate business, either directly or through more persuasive solicitation of the foreign correspondent bank. Another approach in the late 1960s and early 1970s involved minority participations in joint venture or consortium operations with a variety of objectives in a number of overseas locations. With few exceptions, these institutions were found to be inadequate as marketing channels because of the difficulty in establishing the identity of the parent institution through a common vehicle, which was often having a sufficiently difficult time in establishing its own marketing presence.

Having tried a variety of indirect marketing approaches, most medium and large-sized international banks by the mid-1970s became convinced that direct marketing by their own officers was the principal means of establishing their marketing identity and therefore the basis for selling their products. Given the advantage of a physical presence in overseas markets, a bank's representative office, branch and subsidiary network was, therefore, a logical selling force in these markets. A major problem, however, has been to effectively mobilise the overseas staff to sell the product line established in head office. Individuals in representative offices often tend to be isolated from the main business currents of home office, while senior branch and subsidiary officers are obliged by their administrative functions to spend a significant amount of time in non-marketing roles. Such problems have been partially overcome by frequent group marketing sessions designed to communicate selling approaches and resolve individual marketing problems.

In their direct marketing approaches, however, the customer survey described earlier in this chapter has pointed up the apparent failure on the part of many bank calling officers both to do the necessary homework on the corporate prospect and to offer services which are particularly relevant to that prospect. This would appear to reflect the difficulties most banks have had in new product development, as well as the acknowledged shortage of experienced calling officers who can relate their bank's capabilities to a customer's requirements.

In addition to upgrading the quality of calling officers through improved training and recruiting procedures, banks have restructured their international organisations along the lines described in Chapter 5, to bring to bear on the customer or prospect either an industry specialist or an account officer with a global understanding and authority for that particular relationship. Similar steps have been taken to meet the criticism of lack of speed and flexibility of response to a particular customer request, although many of the organisational modifications have created additional problems by frequent changes in account officer, which negate some of the advantages of the new structure.

7 Asset and Liability Management

The purpose of this chapter is to analyse the approach taken by international banking leadership to the management of the portion of their bank's balance sheet for which they have responsibility. Separate volumes in this series deal in detail with loan portfolio management *(International Lending by Commercial Banks,* by T. H. Donaldson) and the management of a bank's foreign exchange and deposit book (*The Money Dealing Function in International Banking,* by Nigel Hudson), two activities which are vital components in the overall management of the asset and liability sides of the international balance sheet. Without unduly duplicating the detailed analysis of these volumes, however, this chapter will take an overall view of the entire international balance sheet from the standpoint of senior international management, with the objective of discussing the policies established by management and the issues with which they deal.

ISSUES IN LIABILITY MANAGEMENT

The evolution of integrated international balance sheet management originates with the Euro-currency interbank foreign exchange and deposit markets based in London in the early 1960s. As mentioned previously, an international bank's initial dealing activities usually commence with meeting customer foreign exchange requirements and funding domestic or international loans. From such essentially matched transactions, banks began to take interest and exchange rate exposures by anticipating changes in these rates, and in many cases significant profits were earned from these positions. In organisations such as US banks with a relatively independent international funding operation, this became a net supplier or taker of funds from the domestic side of the bank, and appropriate 'pool' rates were applied to this net flow. In addition to these funding operations, domestic banks began in the 1960s to price their loans to overseas customers on a floating rate or LIBOR basis, which necessitated bidding for such floating rate deposits in the interbank market.

One series of issues posed by this new market related to the operations of a bank's dealing room which had responsibility for funding the bank's Euro-currency loans, maintaining its presence in the interbank market and generating a profit from its operations. First, in the sector of foreign exchange, management became aware of the distinction between an essentially covered or riskless transaction in connection with a matching trade, and an uncovered position where the dealer was actually at risk and pitting his judgement of interest rate and currency movements against the market. The movement away from central-bank-defended fixed parities in the early 1970s significantly increased the level of uncertainty in a market which heretofore had often been able to profit from a one-way option. Moreover, the natural human instinct of dealers to take advantage of what they considered profit opportunities led to the taking of positions in spot and forward exchange which often had little or nothing to do with customers' or the bank's own requirements. Position limits—by currency, spot and forward—as well as reporting systems were, therefore, designed to measure profitability and ensure that those limits were maintained. Factors such as the counterpart's net worth, the bank's own level of activity and personal relationships went into the fixing of the limits. While such limits and controls existed from the outset in most international banks, they were often ignored or circumvented—sometimes with the concurrence of managements which placed an extraordinary amount of confidence in their dealer's ability to turn a profit—until a series of various well-publicised losses in 1974 from unauthorised dealing and overtrading so shocked the market that elaborate control mechanisms were established and enforced throughout the international banking sector.

A second issue was that of liquidity. By their nature, banks are engaged in the business of maturity transformation; i.e. converting relatively short-term deposits into comparatively longer-term loans and other assets. While in their domestic lending business a major portion of assets in the form of overdrafts and advances are at least nominally of short-term maturity, in the Euro-currency market the contractual maturity of loans extended to ten years or more with the result that the average life of a typical Euro-currency loan portfolio is several years or longer, but is being funded to a preponderant extent by wholesale money market deposits with an average maturity of several months.

The consequent vulnerability of international banks to the inability to renew these deposits was magnified by the practice of mismatching, or short funding, rollover deposit maturities to obtain the profit from funding at a lower cost than the stated rate on the asset financed. While this practice might involve increasing the average maturity of deposits if the dealer predicted an increase in interest rates, more often it meant taking shorter-term deposits in view of the upward-sloping yield curve for longer maturities which normally exists in the major Euro-currency markets.

While unable to eliminate the liquidity threat, international banks have taken a variety of steps to minimise liquidity risk. The most obvious is to present to major depositors—principally other banks—an image of total conservatism and to maintain close personal relationships with such bank and non-bank depositors. Depositor confidence is a vital element in any banking operation, but the unusual dependence of international banks on money market funds and the absence of an obvious international lender of last resort, mean that exceptional measures must be taken to retain the confidence of major depositors. Relatively new entrants to the Euro-currency market, regardless of size or position in their domestic market, thus build up their Euro-currency business gradually as lines are made available to them by established banks. Such efforts received new impetus following the Herstatt crisis of confidence in 1974 when funds tended to flow to the largest, best known and presumably safest institutions at the expense of the smaller, newer and other banks which were perceived as carrying a higher level of depositor risk.

A second policy has been to attempt to quantify a bank's ability to tap the international market, and in this context to establish limits on the extent to which assets are mismatched for given periods of time on a rollover basis. Efforts are also made to avoid over-dependence on one or a group of depositors and to build up the level of customer-related deposits which are presumed to be less volatile because of the closer relationship with the bank. Often elaborate mismatch or gap limits thus limit the extent to which a bank must have recourse to the interbank market for a given period to fund such maturity gaps. In addition, limits in terms of absolute amount and maturity are placed on mismatch positions from a profit and loss standpoint to minimise the extent a bank can be exposed to adverse interest rate movements.

Thirdly, international banks have established liquidity reserves in the form of negotiable instruments and other assets which can be mobilised in the event of difficulties in renewing deposits. In some cases, standby facilities from friendly or related institutions are utilised to supplement these reserves. Finally, international banks have been able to issue negotiable dollar-denominated certificates of deposit and floating rate notes with a contractual maturity approaching or equivalent to that of their loan portfolio. While such issues can only represent a fraction of the total loan book, they do reduce the liquidity exposure significantly, and the banking authorities of many countries outside the US have encouraged their national institutions to undertake such issues. Given the extent of dependence of most international banks on money market funds, however, it is recognised that such measures in the face of a total inability to renew deposits can provide liquidity only for a limited period of time, following which any necessary support must be obtained from central bank or other outside sources.

One possible solution to liquidity problems which is adopted only *in extremis* is the paying of a premium over the appropriate market interest rate to obtain funds. While there can be some disagreement as to the appropriate rate for any given bank at a particular time, the market is extraordinarily sensitive to banks perceived to be paying 'over the odds' for funds, a phenomenon which, particularly in periods of high market tension as in 1974, is interpreted to imply that the particular institution is in difficulty. Such self-fulfilling prophecies probably did occur in the post-Herstatt tension, and banks—particularly the smaller and newer institutions—have gone to great lengths to avoid what they regard as tarnishing their name through overbidding for funds.

These issues of profit and liquidity risk from deposit mismatching in the Euro-currency market are even more difficult to resolve in the case of those banks operating abroad in national money markets, which do not have the breadth of such Euro-currencies as the Euro-dollar, Euro-Deutschemark and Euro-Swiss Franc. As overseas banks have been attracted by the profit potential of lending in local currency to customers in such countries as France, Germany and the UK, they are faced at least initially with almost total dependence for deposits on a local interbank market often dominated by a handful of large national banks who are not only their natural competitors, but who also use this market largely as a safety valve for excess funds. This safety valve can obviously be turned off when money is tight. Such markets are often comparatively new and thus offer relatively short maturities and are capable of violent movements as a result of change in local monetary conditions. In such instances, international banks generally resort to back-up support lines from local institutions as well as absolute controls on exposure to these markets.

A related issue is the problem of access to dollars for non-dollar based banks. The US dollar, as the world's principal reserve currency, as well as the natural choice of the American banks which have played the dominant role in the Euro-currency market, remains the currency of denomination of most Euro-currency loans. The reliance on the Euro-currency inter-bank market to fund a large portfolio of dollar-denominated loans has seriously inhibited many non-dollar-based banks from expanding their international operations. Over time, however, such banks have been able to establish direct US operations through branching and acquisition, and have also gained greater confidence in their ability as a prominent international institution to tap the Euro-dollar market even in time of crisis. The ability of virtually all international banks to attract dollars, even in the very serious psychological crisis of the Herstatt period, has thus quietened some of these concerns.

Another issue relating to dealing operations is the growing complexity and possible duplication which arises as an international bank expands its overseas network of branches and affiliates, each of which may have a separate dealing function. While each operating unit of the network may have its own loan portfolio to fund and a certain amount of local currency business to transact, the great bulk of the business of the dealing room of the typical overseas branch is in exchange and deposit trading in the major Euro-currencies. From a purely intellectual standpoint it should be possible to restrict the size and nature of each unit's money and exchange book to meeting the specific funding and other operations of that particular unit. However, in the real world it is difficult to attract and motivate good dealers whose sole role, for example, might be to fund customer and branch loan requirements on a purely matched basis, while global mismatch positions are taken elsewhere in the bank. In many cases such units can justify taking positions locally on the basis of their particular skills, local market conditions and the particular advantage of their time zone. On balance, however, most banks with extensive Euro-currency dealing operations have moved towards a structure whereby the principal deposit and foreign exchange exposures are taken in one or a limited number of financial centres often on the basis of shifting their position from one time zone to another to maximise profit opportunities and improve co-ordination. Other dealing units are then given quite restricted limits, presumably related primarily to local requirements. This structure does not prevent, however, dealers' natural competitive instincts from attempting to maximise local unit profitability through dealing often in competition or at variance with other units of their bank.

A related organisational issue for many banks is the relationship between, on the one hand, Euro-currency and other international money dealing and, on the other, purely domestic money market operations. For Continental European banks organised along functional lines which have a fully integrated treasury function incorporating both domestic and international operations, this is not a problem. For US and other institutions organised primarily on a territorial basis, however, there are growing pressures to integrate at least the funding operations on a world-wide basis to take maximum advantage of arbitrage possibilities between the domestic currency and its Euro-equivalent, and minimise duplication of effort. The continuing existence in the early and mid-1970s of a higher rate of interest on equivalent maturity Euro-dollars over domestic US dollar deposits and CDs, is one example of the profit opportunities available to US and other banks who can borrow funds in the US and lend them on a matched basis in London or other countries.

At the personnel level, the decision by many US banks to transfer key senior Euro-currency dealers to home office not only increased the level of dealing skills there, but also tended to decrease the level of interbank competition and duplication of effort among their various dealing rooms throughout the world.

Over time, a number of US and other institutions have thus brought an increasing portion of their global balance sheet under unified management. Often supervised by an assets/liabilities management committee, such a management group makes bank-wide decisions as to level and location of mismatch, foreign exchange positions, arbitrage policy, choice and maturity of liabilities (such as Federal Funds, Certificates of Deposit and time deposits) for funding purposes, level and composition of liquidity, extent and location of fixed rate lending, and other judgements on the basis of common assumptions of interest and exchange rate movements. Whether this function remains within the international area of a bank is largely a matter of the relative skills and influence of the key individuals involved, as well as the relative importance of international funding to the bank. In the process of thus breaking down the barriers between international and domestic market operations, banks have often discovered significant new profit opportunities through the integrated management of the bulk of their assets and liabilities. Not only are arbitrage operations facilitated and new opportunities exploited through better human communications, but also senior management has been able to make more efficient use of its overall balance sheet because of the greater degree of integration. Global rather than solely international levels of mismatch can now be determined so that management, having determined its view of interest rates, can establish not only the overall extent of its currency and asset mismatch, but also in which markets it will take these positions.

Despite such progress, however, international bank management continues to face several problems in the management of its overall money dealing functions. In many banks, the management information system is not capable of breaking down the component portions of a deposit and foreign exchange dealing function: the pure matched deposit profit on a back-to-back deposit transaction; the profit derived from a deposit gap or mismatch position; and the pure foreign exchange profit resulting either from favourable movements in spot and forward rates or from a matched transaction. A related concern is the high absolute volume of dealing transactions coupled with the general admission that no control system can totally eliminate the possibility of fraudulent or excessive dealing. While such systems have been imposed over time, one of the continuing risks of the Euro-currency market is the possibility of such dealing losses which occur before management can take appropriate action.

Another problem is that of communication between management and dealers. With the exception of a limited number of individuals who have actually spent several years or more on the trading desk, few international bank managers, from the level of branch manager upward, have a complete understanding of the actual functioning of a dealing room and the nature of the risks and rewards involved in running dealing positions. By the same token, dealers tend to be understandably preoccupied with what is a very high tension, results-oriented profession, and often have difficulty in accepting bank policies which may have a negative effect on their own area of operations. In such an environment, there is often a reluctance to be totally open with management if the dealer feels it will impair his ability to perform. Given the vast sums and potential risks involved, improved communications and mutual understanding between the two is of prime importance to senior bank management.

ISSUES IN ASSET MANAGEMENT

With regard to the portion of the balance sheet controlled by a bank's lending function, management must address a different set of issues. Given the importance of a bank's loan portfolio to its market image and earning power, policies established with regard to the lending function understandably dominate these asset-related issues.

As the typical bank's international portfolio has evolved from virtually riskless short-term loans to medium-term credits involving corporate risks, and eventually to the predominance of long-term loans of a sovereign risk character, there has been a similar evolution of controls over the loan portfolio. One of the principal themes of such controls has been diversification of risk, a traditional banking tenet but one which has special relevance in the international market because of the relative novelty to banks of extensive sovereign risk exposure. The typical international bank will, therefore, have established limits to individual country exposure which will often be broken down further by maturity (short versus medium term), public sector versus private sector, nature of exposure (local currency versus Euro-currency) and so forth. In fixing such limits, banks usually establish some relationship with their own net worth or overall loan portfolio. Similar limits may be applied to specific industries or sectors such as real estate or shipping which carry a perceived level of generic credit risk. Some of the larger and more sophisticated American banks also limit their particular share of bank loans to a given country so as to avoid the vulnerability which might result from being by far the largest lender among overseas banks, should that country have difficulties.

In addition, many banks establish overall loan portfolio guidelines with respect to average loan maturity and the percent of the portfolio which will mature annually so as to ensure a relatively even portfolio run-off. Those banks which engage in fixed rate medium-term lending without the presence of a matching fixed rate deposit generally place overall limits on this form of term mismatch.

The credit decision-making process which has evolved over time reflects the factors of relative bank size and level of international sophistication, the tradition of decision-making within the bank, the personality and influence of key individuals in this process, and past credit experience. One of the distinguishing characteristics of this process is the presence or absence of a credit committee which vets individual exposures prior to approval. The alternative to this collective decision-making process is a delegation of lending authority to individual banking officers in home office and abroad on the basis of their relative position in the organisation and presumed ability to evaluate credits. Most banks provide officers in the field with some delegated lending authority, but in many cases the level of this authority reflects the retail orientation of the bank and is not of an amount—say $1 million or more—sufficient to commit to a typical Euro-currency transaction.

SPECIFIC RESPONSES TO LENDING ISSUES

Of the 38 banks in the questionnaire sample who expressed a specific view, 25 or roughly two-thirds place primary reliance on a credit committee at either the international or bank-wide level in the organisation, while the remaining third delegate most credit decisions to individuals or use a balanced combination of both. US and Canadian banks tend to rely to a greater extent than others on delegation to individual officers: only 57 per cent of those institutions interviewed used a credit committee extensively, while roughly three-quarters of the non-North American banks did so. Not unexpectedly the institutions which characterised themselves as centralised decision-making structures tended also to rely on credit committees, although in a few instances a centralised bank would rely on individual limits and a decentralised one would use a committee system.

Most banks, in particular the larger ones, tend to have two or more levels of credit decision-making authority whether or not a committee system is utilised. A typical pattern would involve a branch or division manager, the head of international and a bank-wide credit committee each taking the ultimate decision on a credit depending upon its size and nature. The overseas manager might have a $1 million lending limit, and his superior in the international function one of $5 million, above which the credit committee must be consulted. The largest US institutions have generally found it necessary from both the administrative and customer service point of view to delegate significant credit authority to officers abroad. By delegating very substantial lending authority to individuals in direct contact with customers, they hope to minimise the inevitable delays associated with presenting a credit at head office. Non-American banks, however, tend to delegate relatively little authority regardless of their size. Aware of the necessity of providing a quick and constructive response to customers, particularly in a highly competitive market, these banks generally take pride in what they regard as a quick 'turnaround' response to a request for credit. As discussed previously in Chapter 4, one-quarter of the banks interviewed cited speed and flexibility of decision-making as the principal element in their business strategy, while the same characteristic was mentioned as one of their three most important strategic elements by a larger number of banks —28—than any other priority.

Whether their customers and the banks offering them loan participations would agree that this strategy has been translated into performance, however, is another question. While an international bank—particularly one utilising credit committees—may feel it has provided a timely response, the period before the customer (or agent bank) receives the desired commitment may be delayed considerably because of the need to communicate complete information to the individual in home office who will present the proposal to the committee, requests for clarification or modification from the committee which must be acted upon in the field, delays in bringing the committee together, and similar factors. The initial enthusiasm of the overseas account officer responsible for the proposal may well give the customer or agent bank an unduly positive impression which often disappears when more senior officers have had the opportunity to apply other points of view to the transaction. For traditional relationships and high priority customers, however, even the largest and most centralised institution can probably give a response within a day or so to a fairly straightforward credit request. Should a complex transaction, new country risk, deviation from standard lending policy or similar factor be involved, a substantially longer response time is involved.

The collective credit decision-making process of most Continental European and Japanese banks differs significantly from that of the typical North American and British institution. Although some exceptions to this generalisation exist, one can say that the majority of Japanese and European banks utilise part or all of their senior management in the form of a Comité de Direction, Vorstand or similar managing body as a credit committee to make the bulk of their credit decisions. Such a diffuse, collective credit responsibility contrasts sharply with the emphasis on individual credit responsibility characteristic of an American, Canadian or British bank whether or not a credit committee is involved in the final decision.

Informal as well as formal procedures characterise the international credit decision-making process. A German Landesbank, for example, may have an elaborate structure of delegation of authority and required approvals from various bodies through the Board of Directors, but many credit decisions are made informally by a very few individuals who secure retrospective approval from the required bodies as needed. Within a given credit committee or level of individual credit responsibility, the authority of individual officers varies widely. Credit committee meetings may be dominated by a chief executive or a senior bank credit officer, while individual officers, depending on personality, experience and influence within the organisation, may either exceed their nominal authorities without fear of retribution or, on the other hand, consult with superiors on credits well within their authority.

A distinction must also be made between different types of credit. While accustomed to evaluating the creditworthiness of other banks, many institutions with relatively new international functions have had little corporate credit background, with the result that experienced domestic banking officers, either through membership of a bank-wide credit committee or as the final lending authority, become involved when an international corporate credit is presented. In most Continental European and Japanese banks which traditionally have had a single (domestic) lending function, this latter continues to make corporate lending decisions even if the customer has been brought in by the international function. Where such lending authority should lie is a subject of some debate among bankers. The larger American banks have built up over time a strong corporate credit capability in their international departments, but smaller institutions in many cases have transferred international corporate lending authority effectively back to domestic officers. Sovereign risk lending is generally the responsibility of international bankers, but in some Japanese, Swiss and other banks this authority resides in a bank-wide lending function. By utilising a bank-wide committee as opposed to one composed of international personnel, management can tailor its approval mechanism to the type of credit involved and the particular strengths and weaknesses of its lending officers.

Another distinction is that of the corporate form of the unit making the credit proposal. Wholly-owned subsidiaries as well as joint ventures and consortium banks tend to receive a greater degree of delegated credit authority than a branch. A number of French, Belgian, American and other banks have utilised wholly-owned subsidiaries rather than branches in overseas markets to perform specific roles, and credit decisions of such institutions may require only a telephoned or telexed approval of a given transaction from home office as opposed to the formal presentation which otherwise might be required.

If a committee system is utilised, it can fulfil a variety of functions in addition to that simply of approving credits. A review committee may evaluate past decisions delegated to individual lending officers on the basis of creditworthiness as well as conformity with bank policy. A credit committee may also set pricing, quality and other lending policies. Finally, it may serve as a vehicle to communicate such policies and to educate officers who are not normally involved in the lending process.

The particular credit decision-making structure chosen by a given bank reflects the latter's overall decision-making approach, which in turn, as previously mentioned, is a function of size and sophistication, the bank's track record, and the personalities and backgrounds of key individuals. A regional bank with a highly domestic-oriented Board of Directors or Chief Executive is quite unlikely to delegate significant credit authority beyond a few trusted individuals, while the same is true of an organisation with a past record of loan losses or other international problems. By the same token, a Continental European or Japanese bank with a tradition of collective decision-making in all sectors will probably want to approve most significant credit decisions at the Board of Management level. On the other hand, management with long experience—and frustration—of operating overseas will tend to delegate more to branches and other units.

THE LOSS RECORD IN INTERNATIONAL LENDING

The presumed principal objective of these procedures and guidelines is, of course, the minimisation of international loan losses over the long term. Apart from US banking institutions which are required to disclose detailed information about the loss experience and other features of their international portfolio, few international banks publicly provide such data. Given the relatively limited legal reporting requirements outside the US and the understandable desire of bankers not to voluntarily advertise past errors, it is unlikely that this situation will change radically in the foreseeable future. It is interesting to note, however, that virtually all of the 40 banks interviewed in this questionnaire sample reported that their historical international loss experience had been nominal or non-existent and therefore only a fraction of the domestic percentage loss ratio, which tends to confirm the experience of the banks which have actually published their loss performance.

An analysis of the published data on US bank international loan loss experience is, nonetheless, a most useful guide to that of the overall industry. Not only do such banks represent close to one-half of the international lending market, but as the leaders and principal innovators of the Euro-currency sector their portfolios can be expected to be relatively mature and reflect most of the risks currently being assumed by such institutions. Table 7.1 provides a comparison of the 1971–7 international versus overall loss experience of seven major US banks. Although the gap has narrowed since 1975, international losses have remained well below bank-wide averages. In the five years to 1975, they ran around one-third of the consolidated level, and in only three instances over this period did a bank's international losses exceed its consolidated average. In the peak international loss year of 1976, the seven banks averaged international write-offs of 0.41 per cent of outstanding against a consolidated average of 0.67 per cent.

TABLE 7.1. International and Consolidated Loan Loss (as percentage of outstandings) Experience of Seven Major US Banks, 1971–7

International	1971	1972	1973	1974	1975	1976	1977
BankAmerica Corp.	0.18	0.10	0.08	0.09	0.10	0.16	0.32
Citicorp	0.18	0.16	0.26	0.35	0.54	0.60	0.39
Chase Manhattan Corp.	0.26	0.14	0.13	0.18	0.24	0.75	0.66
J. P. Morgan	0.00	0.00	0.05	0.00	0.10	0.11	0.08
Manufacturers Hanover Corp.	0.06	0.04	0.01	0.00	0.02	0.00	0.01
Bankers Trust N.Y. Corp.	0.06	0.08	0.18	0.28	0.25	0.25	0.14
Chemical N.Y. Corp.	0.00	0.00	0.00	0.02	0.09	0.10	0.20
Average	0.11	0.07	0.10	0.13	0.19	0.41	0.34
Consolidated							
BankAmerica Corp.	0.27	0.22	0.30	0.28	0.48	0.35	0.25
Citicorp	0.28	0.20	0.32	0.32	0.84	0.79	0.62
Chase Manhattan Corp.	0.37	0.27	0.40	0.37	0.93	1.00	0.68
J. P. Morgan & Co.	0.05	0.06	0.02	0.20	0.63	0.41	0.25
Manufacturers Hanover Corp.	0.22	0.11	0.14	0.47	0.46	0.51	0.37
Bankers Trust N.Y. Corp.	0.55	0.26	0.40	0.56	0.91	0.77	0.70
Chemical N.Y. Corp.	0.36	0.27	0.20	0.26	0.96	0.85	0.57
Average	0.30	0.20	0.25	0.34	0.74	0.67	0.49

Source: Salomon Brothers

A more comprehensive analysis of US bank loss experience in 1977 is provided in a study by Robert Morris Associates summarised in Table 7.2.

TABLE 7.2. Comparison of Domestic and International 1977 Net Loan Charge-offs for US Banks

	Net charge-offs as percentage of average loan portfolio Domestic	International
1. All 751 reporting banks	0.51	—
2. 22 banks with over $5 billion in assets	0.58	—
3. 21 banks with over $5 billion in assets	—	0.185
4. All 127 reporting banks	—	0.176

Source: The Robert Morris Associates

While the sample bases differ, the resulting data do confirm the relatively good performance of international lending for US institutions. In 1977, international write-offs for the broad-based samples were about 0.18 per cent of outstanding loans, or approximately one-third of the domestic loss experience. This relatively low level of international losses was confirmed by the non-US banks interviewed, virtually all of whom reported that their historical international losses were not only low in absolute terms but also in comparison with their respective domestic experience.

The limited available data thus suggest that international loss experience to date has been essentially the result of lending to private firms in sectors and countries which have suffered significant structural problems in the mid-1970s: real estate development throughout the world, large crude oil carrier and bulk cargo ships without adequate time charter revenue, and Mexican private sector firms whose foreign currency borrowings became significantly more expensive following a major devaluation of the peso. The Robert Morris survey quoted above also provides a breakdown of the large losses suffered by US banks internationally in 1977. Of the total $110 million, $23 million, or 21 per cent, had been lent to Mexican private sector entitities. The next largest loss of $16 million related to UK borrowers, principally real estate developers, while the high ranking of Greece, Panama and Liberia reflects shipping losses.

While such experience does in many respects reflect the peculiar nature of international risk, it can be argued that most of these losses were due to factors which caused similar problems in the respective domestic lending sector—overcapacity, inflation, poor management, depressed prices, and so forth.

OUTLOOK FOR INTERNATIONAL LENDING

It is on the future prospects for loss experience, however, that most international bankers focus their attention. Outside observers have pointed out such obvious potential problems as the extremely heavy relative external debt burdens of many developing countries which are not experienced and tested borrowers, the relative immaturity of many banks' international portfolios where grace periods on principal repayments have often not expired, and the very heavy exposure of the banking community as a whole to adverse developments in a limited number of developing countries.

In this context it is particularly interesting to analyse the responses given by the 40-bank sample in connection with the possible extent of future international losses. Of the 31 banks prepared to express a view on the appropriate level of international loan loss reserve for their institution *in the future*, about half considered that a reserve of 0.5 per cent or less of total international loan exposure was appropriate. The remaining half were split roughly between those who considered adequate a reserve of 0.5–1.0 per cent and one of 1.0 per cent and above, Non-North American banks tended to be a bit more conservative, with almost three-quarters advocating a reserve of 0.5 per cent or more against only 40 per cent of the North American institutions.

The sovereign risk and/or bank-guaranteed nature of the bulk of their international portfolios was cited almost unanimously as the justification for a relatively low or nominal international reserve. While most international bankers acknowledge that several smaller sovereign borrowers may go into open default and possibly bring about losses of interest or even principal to the lenders, the point is made that private sector borrowers, both domestic and international, have historically represented far greater risks of actual loss. Many of those interviewed are thus prepared for an increase in the international loss ratio, although only a few felt it would approach domestic levels.

An outside evaluation of the overall international position of a bank's balance sheet is also hindered by the relative lack of publicly-available data. Once again, only US institutions among the major countries provide a breakdown of international assets and liabilities as well as earnings contribution and relative margins. In appraising such vital factors as level of leverage or gearing, liquidity and the ratio of loans to deposits, however, it can be argued that it is irrelevant and artificial to break out the international component of a balance sheet in what is essentially an integrated international institution.

What is of relevance to the management of such institutions, however, is the relative importance of the international component of a bank's earnings and assets. The growth of such aggregates in percentage terms has been impressive enough; but in addition slow growth or stagnation in domestic earnings plus severe domestic setbacks in individual cases have caused the international contribution to earnings to rise in many cases to 50 per cent or more of the bank's total. Of the 34 banks in the questionnaire sample who calculate the overall profit contribution of the international function (six do not or do not feel it is relevant), about one-third show an international contribution ranging from 10–20 per cent of the total, with another fifth in the 30–40 per cent category. Four, or roughly 12 per cent, had an international contribution exceeding 50 per cent of the total. The higher levels have been achieved by the larger US banks which have suffered from flat domestic earnings for many years as well as other banks with major domestic earnings problems.

Of the 37 institutions prepared to hazard an opinion, roughly two-thirds anticipate an increase in their percentage of international earnings over the medium term. About half of the North American banks polled forecast such an increase, while only two of the other seventeen institutions foresaw a decrease in the percentage. There was no particular correlation between the existing level of international contribution and the forecast. Those predicting further relative growth usually foresaw fairly unattractive domestic expansion prospects, while many of those predicting a decline had in mind a recovery or continuation of domestic loan demand. American banks were not optimistic about future international growth because of the relatively unattractive risk/reward ratio prevalent in mid-1978 in the Euro-currency market and the corresponding relative attractiveness of domestic lending. On the other hand, the more optimistic bankers in many cases reflected the amortisation of heavy past expenses of building up their international function which should produce, in the future, more attractive profits.

A very interesting issue is that of whether a limit should be placed on the earnings or asset contribution of the international function to the global bank. Of 34 banks which responded to this query, somewhat less than half saw no need for such a policy determination; they essentially believed that a pragmatic approach should be taken with regard to the relative risk and reward of international business. On the other hand, a small majority felt that considerations of external perception (the stock market, customers, regulatory authorities, etc.) required that the international contribution be limited to a certain percentage of the total. For many European banks, such a constraint stemmed from a desire to be seen to retain a national character or a given domestic market share, while many US institutions are concerned about their image with investors and customers. A frequent maximum contribution cited by many American regional banks is that of one-third of total profits and assets. Many European bankers interviewed criticised US institutions for reaching a level of international earnings which could result in a possible loss of identity, while others have in mind the more material concern of diversification of assets and earnings.

THE REGULATORY FACTOR

The regulatory climate in which an international bank operates is also of keen interest to those responsible for the management of international assets and liabilities. Regulatory approaches by central banking and other institutions responsible for the overseas operations of their national banks vary considerably. In many cases, regulators have taken some time to react to the rapid evolution of the Euro-currency market and its implications for the banks they control. The Herstatt crisis of confidence in 1974, however, focused attention on the risk of loss in international banking, as well as the ultimate responsibility for the support of individual banks, whose rescue might be considered necessary to prevent a spiralling international banking crisis of confidence.

Regulatory responsibility for American banks abroad, which

represent the largest single share of the Euro-currency market, is divided between the Comptroller of the Currency and the Federal Reserve Board. The latter has traditionally focused on the quality of bank assets, and in its detailed examinations of the overseas operations of US banks it continues to evaluate the quality of a given loan portfolio. Its approach to the increased overseas emphasis of US banks over the past decade has been accomodating, although traditionally it has required member banks to apply for approvals for most overseas expansion initiatives, and in recent years it has considerably increased the amount and scope of information it requires on such operations.

The Comptroller of the Currency, however, has adopted a more pragmatic regulatory approach which in recent years has focused on the quality of management and its procedures, policies and controls. While detailed international examinations are regularly conducted, they tend increasingly to rely for primary information on the bank's own review and control procedures as well as those of outside bodies such as auditors. Although the Comptroller's examination thus takes a more comprehensive view which contrasts a bank's own international objectives and strategy with actual results, the agency has taken a number of positions in recent years with regard to categorisation of quality of country risk and the extent of exposure to individual sovereign borrowers which have caused a significant amount of controversy.

The two US agencies have thus adopted quite distinctive and separate regulatory approaches. On the other hand, in recent years efforts to coordinate and mesh these philosophies have resulted in some movement towards common statistical reporting and evaluation of sovereign risk.

The regulatory philosophy of the Bank of England, which supervises not only the international operations of the major British banks but also the plethora of London-based foreign-owned international institutions, is quite different. Focusing its attention on a bank's overall business and its relation to its peer group, the Bank of England places a high priority on the quality of management, market reputation, loss record, and profitability as well as having regard to balance sheet ratios which measure leverage, liquidity, risk assets and other factors. An underlying assumption is trust; credit files are not normally inspected to determine the true quality of assets. The moral suasion imparted by the Bank of England has traditionally exercised a considerable degree of control over internationally-oriented UK banking institutions. In 1974, in the so-called secondary banking crisis, a number of institutions failed, although these were not institutions which fell within the bank's then regular sphere of influence. The introduction of statutory controls over a greater range of banks and the reinforcement of its regulatory staff will supplement this traditional authority.

The Japanese authorities' regulatory approach, while comparable in influence on the banking community with that of the Bank of England, is based on a totally different philosophy. The Ministry of Finance exercises its overall regulatory jurisdiction through the Bank of Japan and is concerned primarily with establishing strict guidelines which will oblige Japanese banks to function in what is seen to be the national interest. Since World War II, therefore, it has promoted the establishment of specialist institutions such as the Bank of Tokyo and various Japanese-owned consortia and joint ventures to fulfill specific functions and test new markets. Through extensive examinations, approvals and balance sheet controls, the regulatory authorities have concerned themselves with such questions as the quality of assets, the orderly expansion of Japanese banks abroad, the rates paid by Japanese banks for funds and the maturity mismatching of their assets so as to avoid any loss of reputation on the part of Japanese institutions internationally and to ensure that the banks act in the Japanese national interest as defined by government policy.

8 The International Banks' Network

A distinguishing feature of the increasing internationalisation of the banking industry in the 1970s has been the proliferation throughout the world of national banks' representative offices, branches, subsidiaries and affiliates. Whereas in previous periods overseas offices were primarily those of 'colonial' banks which provided basic trade-financing services to developing countries, the new breed of such offices post-World War II has had a variety of objectives. The purpose of this chapter is to describe these objectives, analyse the structure and functioning of the networks and discuss how banks are resolving some of the principal issues which emerge from the growth of overseas networks.

THE OBJECTIVES OF A NETWORK

The principal objectives of a network of offices doing international business—some of which can be located in the parent bank's own national market—can be summarised as follows:

Euro-currency interbank market dealing
customer service
base for penetrating new markets
market coverage for existing services
unit profitability

Tapping the Euro-currency market for wholesale deposits and lending out surplus domestic funds were among the original motivations for establishing the initial elements of an overseas network. German and American banks in particular, faced with regulatory restrictions on lending abroad from domestic sources, have found it necessary to use offshore subsidiaries and branches to take in or lend out their national currencies, while other banks have found it more convenient to open branches in London and other Euro-currency centres than participate in this market primarily through their home office. As the Euro-currency market has broadened and become more sophisticated, major banks are finding it useful to run global deposit and foreign exchange positions which are carried from unit to unit in different time zones throughout the world, so that such an integrated position is truly run on a 24-hour-a-day basis.

What is essentially a defensive response to the requirements of existing customers has in the past often been the motivation for opening individual branches and representative offices abroad. Such requirements could range from a retail facility for home country tourists or expatriate workers to one which serviced the local requirements of the overseas subsidiary of a domestic corporate customer. In more recent years, however, as the level of competition and costs have increased, other objectives have taken priority.

Perhaps the principal such objective in today's market is the penetration of what is for the particular bank a new geographic or functional sector. The combination of physical presence in a given market which facilitates doing business with local corporations and governments, the possibility of tapping sources of local currency funds for on-lending, and the ability to compete directly with local banks which an overseas unit makes possible, have motivated hundreds of banks to set up offices in national markets which appear intrinsically attractive. The potential profitability of a particular functional sector such as merchant banking or leasing has offered similar attractions.

Another motive of interest primarily to the larger banks is the drive to increase geographic market coverage so as to offer to customers a more comprehensive and efficient service. Such additional links in an international chain may represent a significant competitive advantage over a local or other foreign bank, which cannot service a customer's world-wide requirements as effectively.

Finally, the great majority of operating units is expected to provide an incremental profit contribution to the bank in addition to meeting one or more of the above objectives. While many decisions to open new offices are made instinctively by the senior management of a bank, in other cases the decision is preceded by an often elaborate feasibility study which projects incremental costs and revenues. The latter are naturally the more difficult to calculate and often do not represent truly incremental earnings but simply an effective transfer from other areas of the bank which have or could have generated them. In institutions such as American banks, which place a high priority on profitability, new operational units such as branches and subsidiaries are expected to generate satisfactory profits for the bank within a reasonable period of time.

THE CHOICE OF VEHICLE

The choice of individual unit or vehicle and the extent of a network are generally dictated by the bank's strategy as well as the obvious considerations of size and international experience of the bank, current availability of human resources, and the nature of the bank's domestic and international business. As these factors evolve along with its international strategy, the bank's attitude towards its network as a whole and the choice of individual units is equally likely to change.

The total absence of an international network presumes a reliance on a bank's own travelling officers, Euro-currency loan participations and overseas correspondent banks as a source of customers, loans and trade-financing opportunities. For relatively small banks without a broad base of experienced management, this solution avoids the expenditure of funds and management time on an overseas network but, correspondingly, does not permit funding access to the Euro-currency market, enable the bank to penetrate new national markets or offer its existing services to potential foreign customers through a locally-based vehicle. A number of smaller national banks have, however, been able to build profitable portfolios of syndicated loan participations and a certain level of trade-related financing without the costly infrastructure of an overseas network.

A representative office—or loan production office, in more recent terminology—represents a relatively low cost effort to achieve the two objectives of customer service and market penetration. Such an office cannot take in or lend funds on its own books and thus permit the parent organisation to participate either in the Euro-currency market or local interbank market, but at least in theory it provides the capability of selling existing services and of generating certain local business which can be booked elsewhere in the network. Banks have found that the annual expenditure of up to several hundred thousand dollars equivalent necessary to run such an office and the relative facility of closing it down, if business prospects so dictate, make it a very useful preliminary step in exploring a new market. On the other hand, in its business development function it is often hampered by its inability to commit for its own account and therefore its reliance on decision-makers elsewhere in the network. There is also the difficulty of attracting to such a position the successful marketing officer who can have a greater impact on an operating vehicle such as a branch. Finally, most banks find it quite difficult to evaluate the performance of an overseas representative whose efforts by definition are reflected in other profit centres throughout the bank. Despite these drawbacks, a number of banks who have posted an energetic, experienced and competent officer in such an office have been most pleased with its cost effectiveness in developing profitable business in contrast with the branch alternative.

A branch, on the other hand, can operate as a legal and functional extension of the head office and therefore participate in money markets and develop local business subject to the constraints of local regulations and conditions and the capabilities of its staff. While the annual operating cost is a multiple of that of the representative office because of the additional space and staffing requirements, there is normally no need to put up a significant amount of capital in local currency, and the branch can deal in the market with the full resources of the parent effectively behind it. Perhaps more important in recent years has been the identity and responsiveness provided by such an extension of the parent as banks have found it absolutely necessary in a highly competitive market to establish their own name and ensure that the network is responsive to the strategy established. One useful by-product of establishing a major branch is the banking and management training it can offer to home office personnel as a banking institution in microcosm.

On the other hand, the annual operating expenses of a branch are significantly more than those of a representative office and, in view of the range and integration of dealing, marketing and other functions carried on, are difficult to reduce without impairing the branch's effectiveness. Another problem often encountered is that a substantial portion of the time of the limited number of experienced branch officers is taken up by management rather than revenue-generating preoccupations. A precondition to achieving the specific objectives of a branch is dealing successfully with the host of regulatory, personnel, cultural, linguistic and business problems associated with doing business in a foreign environment, and the handful of senior expatriate and local banking officers in a branch often has limited time left for actually doing business after dealing with these concerns. Lastly, the presence of a branch network poses significant problems of delegation of authority and possible duplication of functions with other units of a bank's network. To the extent that the initiative and skills necessary to succeed in branch management exist, there may also be real frustration in organisations where little authority is delegated to the field and each unit has a relatively narrow ambit.

A variant of the branch alternative is the wholly-owned subsidiary which may offer a different range of services than those possible through a branch. Home or host country legislation and other factors may thus require the parent organisation to capitalise the vehicle, which may involve a significant local currency exposure which is not present in the case of a branch. American-owned merchant banks outside the US, and Luxembourg subsidiaries of German banks are examples of such capitalised vehicles which perform roles not possible in branch offices because of legal and regulatory constraints. In the case of the former, US regulations prohibiting the carrying on of investment banking activities, such as securities underwriting, oblige US banks to perform these operations through overseas subsidiaries exempt from such constraints, while German banks have chosen offshore subsidiaries so as to avoid ratio and other limitations placed on the activities of branches by German regulations.

A final structural option is the joint venture or consortium institution in which the bank joins with one or more partners to establish a capitalised vehicle in an overseas market. While this alternative does not offer the responsiveness and identity desired by many international banks, it may represent the most practical and realistic option for a bank to penetrate a specific functional or geographic market. In recent years, for example, local regulations in a number of highly attractive markets such as Australia and Spain have effectively required substantial local equity participation as a precondition to entry by a foreign bank. A number of banks have successfully used such a participation as an alternative to a wholly-owned vehicle, particularly during their early international development when they were reluctant to move overseas without the partnership of more experienced institutions who could assist in providing staffing, business development and capital support. In today's market the most successful of these ventures are those which have developed their own management momentum and specialist identity in the market place.

One of the major problems faced by such joint ventures is the evolution over time of individual bank strategies and market conditions which cause adjustment problems often difficult to resolve within the prescribed objectives and fixed shareholdings of the joint company. A consortium which made excellent strategic sense to a group of regional banks in 1970 may, therefore, represent duplication of function in 1978 as the stockholder banks have developed their own Euro-currency business. Another problem which surfaced during the 1974 crisis of confidence is that of ultimate responsibility for funding and depositor liability in the event of serious difficulties. The larger stockholder banks with particular concern for their market reputation often consider that their liability for keeping depositors whole goes well beyond their nominal legal liability as represented by their share of the capital; in such cases they are reluctant to continue as stockholders without the ability to control management performance.

On balance, an interest in a joint venture or consortium thus offers the advantages of partnership with experienced institutions capable of making a contribution to the venture, a relatively low expenditure of capital and management resources in an operating vehicle, and the ability to penetrate markets which local legal or other factors may foreclose to branches and other wholly-owned vehicles. On the other hand, the lack of identity, frequent inability to control management, the possibility of having to bail out other stockholders in the event of a crisis, and the problems which arise when the perceived needs of stockholders change, have significantly reduced the popularity of this alternative since the late 1960s.

THE STRUCTURING OF A NETWORK

The structuring of a network utilising the particular strengths and weaknesses of these types of vehicle involves a careful balancing of a bank's management resources, the potential of given national markets, possible duplication with existing and likely future overseas offices and the nature of a bank's clientele and the service it offers. The initial decisions are usually the easiest: a London or New York branch to provide Euro-currency or dollar funding and develop multinational corporate business in the UK or US; representative offices or branches in major national markets where existing major customers are located or where a bank's specialist expertise is in great demand; and possibly a branch in another major regional market such as Asia to provide funding and incremental business in that region.

As the network expands, however, the decisions become more difficult. Firstly, existing management resources become stretched; the variety of credit, personnel, cultural, marketing and management skills required to successfully manage an overseas unit are found in a limited number of individuals whose services may be better utilised in home office. A bank struggling to develop international corporate lending, marketing and other skills can often not spare such scarce talent to open up a far-off office.

Another people-related problem is the motivation and eventual reabsorption of experienced overseas officers elsewhere in the network. An energetic and competent overseas officer, particularly during periods when international business is regarded by the bank as relatively unattractive, can become quite frustrated if he perceives interesting business opportunities in his local market which are consistently rejected by his superiors in home office. When the time comes for eventual transfer to headquarters, he may regret the loss of the relative degree of authority and responsibility associated with such a transfer to the extent of leaving the bank in order to remain in the market he has come to know.

The understandable practice of using major overseas offices such as London branches as a training ground for high potential senior managers poses additional problems. While a domestically-trained or relatively inexperienced international banker obtains a good deal of useful experience through a two or three-year tour in such an office, what usually suffers is the morale of local staff denied promotional opportunities, as well as customers who, every few years, must deal with a new account officer who is transferred at just about the time he becomes useful to them.

A second problem area relates to the cost and complexity of the administrative apparatus necessary to support a large network of overseas offices. Such an apparatus seems to grow more rapidly than the actual network in terms of expense and claims on management time. As the number of overseas employees rises, a sophisticated personnel infrastructure dealing with a host of compensation, regulatory, transfer, accommodation, tax and other problems becomes necessary. Transfer of officers to and from an offshore location comes to involve a host of decisions as to housing, allowances, compensation, job content and other factors which must be resolved to the individual's reasonable satisfaction to retain his motivation and commitment. Management information systems co-ordinating and controlling the network's dealing and lending functions become more expensive and complex. Procedures must be established, for example, to allocate among different overseas units a global credit limit for individual customers and banks. More management time must be spent in planning, co-ordination and marketing meetings for overseas staff to establish and implement strategic programmes. Once established, this plethora of staff functions is difficult to reduce and tends to grow steadily in cost and complexity.

From a business development and marketing point of view, an expanded network creates real pressures on management to restructure the bank's organisation and decision-making functions to respond more effectively to customer requirements and the natural desire of overseas officers to operate with a greater degree of autonomy. In response to these pressures, the major American banks have either significantly increased the level of authority delegated to the field or reorganised in the direction of the geographic/functional matrix-structures described in Chapter 5. While such restructuring is intellectually satisfying and often quite effective in the marketplace, the disruption caused by such an organisational change and the inevitable increase in time spent on internal co-ordination have gone some way to offset the obvious advantage of a large overseas network.

Perhaps a more serious problem is simply the level of competition in local markets which has built up over time through the arrival of new foreign bânks and their marketing techniques as well as the responses of local institutions. While the first American branches in a market such as the UK or Germany thus profited considerably from relatively unprospected opportunities in a hitherto highly structured market, those banks opening up in these markets in the late 1970s have had a more difficult row to hoe.

Finally, the management of a large and growing network inevitably involves the more precise definition of roles of individual units and attempts to reconcile effective management control with the need to motivate overseas management and compete effectively in the marketplace. In a large and far-flung network, the response of many American and other banks has been to establish regional headquarters with line and/or staff relationships to overseas units in that region. In its ultimate extreme, such a regional headquarters assumes most of the credit and other decision-making authority of home office, whose role is limited to the establishing of world-wide policy guidelines, planning and control of performance. In more limited versions, a large branch or regional office can provide staff support to local units in sectors such as personnel, credit, tax, marketing and accounting.

The success of regional delegation has been a function of the willingness of senior management in home office to truly delegate such line and staff functions, the real and perceived influence and competence of officers at various levels in the field and, of course, the financial and marketing results achieved. It goes without saying that a major loss or other disaster stemming from delegated authority is not conducive to continuation of such delegation. True delegation of line authority, particularly in the lending function, requires a degree of self denial and abstinence on the part of home office staff which, in many cases of active and experienced individuals, is difficult to achieve. Without such real delegation and the implicit home office support that goes with it, however, a regional office may be counter-productive in that it becomes an additional—and often expensive—line in an already long administrative chain, which is increasingly circumvented by officers in the field who naturally seek out the ultimate source of authority. On the other hand, where real delegation of authority in line or staff matters exists and where overseas officers effectively utilise their increased flexibility, the impact on morale, profits and customer satisfaction has been impressive.

SPECIFIC MANAGEMENT RESPONSES

Management interviews in connection with the questionnaire produced some interesting views with regard to networks and their likely future development. While such results inevitably reflect conditions and views as of mid-1978, they do have some validity in a longer term context. Of the 38 banks which characterised their present networks, roughly equal numbers fell into three arbitrarily defined categories as follows:

(i) offices/branches which do *extensive local as well as international* business in a large number of national markets abroad;

(ii) offices/branches in most or all of the world's *leading financial centres* which primarily carry on *international* business; and

(iii) offices/branches only in a *limited* number of offshore centres so as to permit home office *access* to the international market.

In addition, two of the banks fell into the final category:

(iv) no offshore offices beyond a *limited* number of *representatives* who do not do business directly.

While these categorisations are admittedly arbitrary, they do correspond roughly to the articulated expansion strategies of a number of banks. The institutions were then asked to determine whether their network was:

(a) Largely in place (given current market conditions);

(b) some expansion was likely to occur; or

(c) a major network increase was in prospect.

Of the 38 banks responding, 23, or roughly 60 per cent, indicated that their networks were largely in place (a), while another third foresaw some expansion (b). There was no significant differentiation between the sample of American/Canadian banks and the other institutions in terms of likely expansion prospects. Of equal interest is the indication that banks with less developed networks are likely, despite the pressures on profitability which existed in mid-1978, to continue to expand their overseas operations. Of the 12 banks in category (i)—the largest and most sophisticated networks—only one-third predicted any marked level of further expansion (categories b and c), while of the 13 institutions in category (iii)—a limited number of units to provide market access—roughly two-thirds foresaw such a likely increase.

These admittedly fragmentary results would appear to support external evidence indicating that, almost regardless of nationality and current market conditions, banks developing their international networks follow an almost predictable pattern within an overall strategic plan. The need for, say, a Tokyo branch or a New York office is regarded as a strategic requirement which hopefully can be justified financially under current market conditions. While a relatively mature bank may thus be agonising over whether to close an office in a given market because of a poor profit outlook, a less advanced competitor may be about to open one across the street.

THE PROBLEM OF COST EFFECTIVENESS

Another set of questions revealed some interesting insights into the role played by quantifiable results in the decisions to open, operate and possibly close an overseas office. While virtually all banks interviewed analyse the potential profitability of a proposed overseas operating unit such as a branch or affiliate, a sharp division of attitude is shown when it is assumed, for purposes of argument, that an existing operating unit is demonstrably unlikely to produce, directly or indirectly, satisfactory quantifiable results for the bank as a whole. Faced with what is seen to be a source of future overall losses over an extended period of time, roughly half of the US and Canadian banks interviewed would be prepared to close down a branch or other operating unit despite the possible damage of such a closure to its reputation and the difficulty of re-entering that national market at a future point in time. None of the non-North American institutions, however, would be prepared to take such an action, arguing that a longer-term and non-financial view must be taken of the attractiveness of the given market, government and customer relationships and the possible damage to a bank's image.

A different attitude is often shown towards representative offices which are seen to be less visible overseas outposts with less easily quantifiable outputs. American and other banks alike often regard these less expensive units as a necessary customer and marketing service whose results do not have to be quantified. On the other hand, should market conditions change or perceived results prove disappointing, a much larger proportion of banks is prepared to close down a representative office. A similar pragmatic approach is taken towards minority interests in consortium banks; a fairly large proportion of banks around the world has no hesitation about selling out of a consortium—if possible—if given profit and other objectives are not achieved.

Such a pragmatic viewpoint on the part of American banks in particular reflects not only their greater concern with overall, long term profitability, but also the rising cost level associated with maintenance of an overseas network. The relative decline of the dollar against a number of currencies in the mid-1970s has focused further attention on the general vulnerability of a personnel-intensive service operation in an inflationary world. With upwards of two-thirds of a typical unit's non-interest costs related to staff and their compensation, international banks have suffered particularly from the rise in wage levels and fringe benefits throughout the world in the 1970s. Premises expense on rented quarters, particularly in prestige locations, has equally sky-rocketed. In addition, the mounting cost of indirect expense—computerisation, personnel and other new staff functions—needed to maintain an increasingly sophisticated operation has also contributed to the inflation of operating expenses.

Profit-conscious institutions have, therefore, become increasingly concerned with the cost effectiveness of a given overseas network. Marketing, funding and competitive pressures have in many cases reinforced the need for an effective overseas network, which increases the difficulty of reducing the level of expense growth without impairing the network's effectiveness. Representative offices in secondary markets have often been closed or transformed, through a change in personnel and nomenclature, into a 'loan production office' whose objectives are more closely attuned to the generation of incremental revenue than the passive 'servicing' of existing relationships. While the closing of a branch in a significant market area is a painful and usually deferrable decision, some American banks have reduced cost levels by moving to less prestigious premises, cutting out certain functions, such as retail banking, which are seen to be relatively unprofitable, and rationalising certain dealing operations which can be eliminated or carried on elsewhere in the network.

For even the most profit-conscious banks, however, the non-financial considerations involved in closing overseas offices in major market centres such as London often swing the decision. A number of international heads of regional banks interviewed have recommended such closure to senior management which has not concurred because of considerations relating to personal and corporate prestige, and the decision to take a longer-term view in spite of the acknowledged lack of utility of the office in the bank's present international posture. In a number of cases, the difficulty of quantifying a unit's overall contribution and the commitment of key individuals in an organisation reinforce the natural reluctance to be seen to be retrenching. On the other hand, a significant number of American banks feel that, properly explained to the outside world in terms of the constructive need to divert resources elsewhere in the network, the announcement of closing an office can have a net positive impact on a bank's market standing.

European and Japanese banks, however, are quick to criticise what can be regarded as a short-sighted decision, and they quote the number of instances when US and other banks have pulled out of markets under difficult conditions and thereby significantly impaired their ability to re-enter when the market became more attractive. Most major Continental European banks went so far in the interviews as to state that they would only close an operating unit overseas if literally forced to by external conditions such as nationalisation or civil conflict.

ATTITUDES TOWARDS CONSORTIA

Finally, responses to the questionnaire with regard to attitudes toward joint ventures and consortium institutions confirmed evidence in 1977 and 1978 of a marked swing of interest away from such participations. Of the 38 banks responding, only 7, or 18 per cent, considered that a joint venture or consortium participation was a useful option which should play a role in their overseas strategy. The remaining responses varied from an absolute prohibition on such participations to the statement that an uphill fight would be necessary to sell such a venture within the bank. Most banks acknowledged that local regulations and market conditions might necessitate the use of a specific joint venture or consortium approach, but the distinct preference among at least four-fifths of the banks was to find a solution which at least permitted them to retain overall management control, if not 100 per cent ownership, of a venture whose role was carefully defined, with partners who were certain to be compatible and make a significant contribution.

The predominantly negative attitudes towards less than 100 per cent ownership of a vehicle stem not only from the general factors discussed previously in this chapter—an evolution of strategy, the greater emphasis on network identity and responsiveness, etc.—but also direct experience in individual consortia and joint ventures. While some of these institutions have made notable progress in profit generation and market impact, the majority have shown a relatively unimpressive return on capital and assets. More to the point, in some cases parent banks have suffered actual losses and/or damage to their image from support provided to affiliates requiring funding or transfer of bad loans to remain viable.

Many bankers admit, however, that attitudes to joint ventures ebb and flow, and that such emotion in mid-1978 was particularly negative. What many bankers tend to forget is the utility of such a participation to less mature institutions and, in fact, to their own at a given point in the past. It is easy to forget that a relative newcomer to the international scene may very justifiably select a joint venture or minority participation as an alternative to a branch or representative office as an initial step into the Euro-currency market.

The problems tend to arise over time as individual strategies and market conditions evolve and it becomes institutionally difficult to restructure or otherwise modify an entity which has also generated its own personality and momentum. It is also evident that, with perfect hindsight, the long-term compatibility of partners and strategy of the joint venture vehicle was, in many cases, not sufficiently thought out. The fact remains, however, that roughly one-fifth of the banks interviewed profess themselves essentially pleased with their existing consortium and joint venture interests and would positively consider new ones.

9 Performance Measurement

Having examined how international banks establish objectives and structure organisations, marketing programmes, asset/liability management and networks to achieve these objectives, it is now appropriate to determine how and to what extent actual performance of the international function is monitored and action taken, if necessary, to achieve stated objectives. Such performance measurement can take the form not only of profitability statistics but also quantification of other results such as amount of new business generated, performance of service departments and so forth.

DEBATE OVER IMPORTANCE OF PERFORMANCE MEASUREMENT

The need for performance measurement itself is a matter of some debate among international bankers. At the one extreme are a number of large American banks with highly sophisticated, profit-oriented information systems which go as far as measuring the incremental return on capital or assets of each individual loan transaction proposed. To such institutions, banking is a business like any other whose ultimate objective is to maximise long term profitability for stockholders, and each operating unit, function and significant transaction must be evaluated with this objective in mind. A total of seven such banks in the questionnaire sample, for example, have highly refined formulae which assume a given level of loss reserve and capital allocation to support each domestic and international loan submitted for approval. Unless a minimum return on capital or assets is generated by the revenues produced from the proposed transaction, or the loan officer can justify the transaction on the basis of a strong relationship, the proposal is presumably rejected. Behind such formulae lie detailed calculations of a bank's appropriate level of leverage, dividend payout, desired return on net worth and allocation of capital and loss reserves, not only to the various functions of the bank but also to different categories of assets.

At the other extreme are institutions such as many Japanese and Continental European banks for whom incremental profits, however measured, are only one of a number of objectives for their institution. Such goals may include a strong commitment to contributing to the perceived national interest, maintenance of market share, a genuine belief that they are a service institution one of whose major objectives is to assist traditional customers in international dealings, and a concern for fairness to employees, community service and professionalism which could easily conflict with the profit motive.

Quite apart from such fundamental philosophical differences are the practical problems of measuring performance in a complex organisation subject to a variety of exogenous factors beyond management's control. Many international bankers honestly object to profit measurement in an industry whose fortunes are subject to government intervention, monetary policy and interest rate levels, loan demand, level and volatility of foreign exchange activity as well as the elements of civil strife, war and other characteristics of international business. Moreover, in an industry where losses on the loan portfolio and foreign exchange book can threaten the existence of the bank itself, such critics feel that setting income targets which imply a given level of credit or foreign exchange risk could well motivate lending officers and dealers to make commitments regardless of market conditions, simply to fulfil a given profit target.

At the level of the individual institution, a much larger proportion of bankers consider that the necessarily arbitrary classifications of revenues, expenses, loan reserves and capital funds needed for a thorough-going evaluation of the international function effectively negate the value of the results obtained. The fundamental decision to assign revenue and costs to international, as opposed to domestic operations, is to many a totally illogical distinction, in view of their image of the international function as representing one of the many customer services going to make up an overall package which cannot be broken up for analysis.

Of more concern to many managers are the practical problems both of designing a management information system to provide relevant data, and of making the arbitrary allocations of certain overhead costs and capital to the respective banking functions. Honest managers can disagree honestly over such knotty questions as the level of a bank's capital necessary to support a given asset such as interbank loans, the appropriate allocation of loan loss reserves to sovereign risk credits, and the proportion of senior management overhead to be allocated to the international function. In addition, particularly in European and other banks where major domestic branches carry on an active international business quite apart from the central international function, there are real practical problems and costs of actually delineating the related expenses and revenues associated with international business in such branches or operating centres.

Underlying many of these logical argements, however, are highly subjective views stemming from the personal motives of the individuals involved. An international banker may be unlikely to support detailed performance measurement if it would reveal the relative unprofitability of his own function or department, while there is a natural reluctance on the part of many individuals to commit themselves to a given level of performance as part of a plan target. By the same token, in the case of institutions committed to performance measurement, motives other than an honest search for the statistical truth may be behind such a commitment. In the US, stockholder and regulatory requirements have obliged banks to calculate and often publish data which the bankers involved would clearly love to remain a state secret. Moreover, for an international function performing well and showing a satisfactory rate of growth compared to its domestic counterpart, it is understandable that the individuals in question should seek to quantify their performance.

For the objective observer, however, the reasonable approach to international bank performance measurement probably lies somewhere between the two extremes. To those objecting to the importance of external variables in determining bank performance, the proper response is to isolate as many key exogenous variables, such as interest and exchange rates, as possible, and establish agreed bank-wide planning assumptions which can be modified, along with plan targets, as appropriate.

To those concerned about the arbitrary aspects of planning as a management process, it should be pointed out that planning is part of a strategic process designed to achieve long-term objectives, not simply to punish or reward individuals on the basis of short term performance. If a given function year after year fails to perform as projected, such performance may well be attributable to an incorrect strategic decision or assumption, rather than the competence and commitment of the individuals performing the function.

Finally, to those objecting to the arbitrariness of allocations of capital and loss reserves as well as items of cost and revenue, the proper response is to consider the importance of the international function in many banks in relation to the possible error which may stem from an unreasonable assumption in the allocation process. In banks with billions of dollars equivalent in international loans outstanding, thousands of international employees and dozens of overseas offices, performance measurement must make sense. If a given variable such as overhead or capital allocation is perceived to be critical to the decision-making process, it should be isolated and a range of possible outcomes should be assumed to determine the extent to which the actual decision-making process might be influenced.

HOW PERFORMANCE IS MEASURED

While it is impossible to quantify the extent to which international banks review profit performance against plan and actually take action in the light of this performance, the available evidence indicates that a relatively small minority of the total universe of such banks—primarily US institutions—use actual results against plan as a basis of action to achieve strategic objectives. For most banks, planning and performance measurement is primarily a statistical exercise. Adverse results tend to be attributed to factors beyond the bankers' control such as absence of loan demand or inactivity in the exchange markets, and thorny decisions with regard to closing units and functions or removing low performers from positions they have long held are fudged or deferred. On the other hand, a limited number of banks have not hesitated to take difficult structural and personnel decisions in the light of below-par performance.

The actual measurement of profit performance can take a

variety of forms. The first is measurement of the profits of a given department or branch, which is a relatively simple exercise in view of the identifiable revenues and costs associated with a function which is effectively an operating unit. More difficult, however, is measuring the profitability of a given product or service which may or may not produce identifiable revenues and often cannot be costed without highly arbitrary allocations of expense. Another difficult area for many banks is analysing the profitability of the funds management or money dealing function so as to isolate the various components of a dealing room's contribution—earnings from matched deposits, mismatched deposits, matched foreign exchange and mismatched foreign exchange positions.

Perhaps most difficult and frustrating of all is the measurement of customer profitability: the bringing together of all world-wide revenues earned from a customer and the expenses associated with those revenues. Few accounting systems are geared for such analysis, which is particularly vital in dealing with centralised multinational corporate customers who have a very precise idea of what they are giving and receiving from each of their banks and do not hesitate to negotiate the best possible deal on the basis of presumed overall benefits from the relationship.

To a great extent, the difference in approach to performance measurement reflects traditional techniques of management. Japanese and Continental European institutions have, as pointed out in Chapter 6, historically been run on a collective or consensus basis, and organisational structures and accounting systems have reflected this bias. For such an institution to pinpoint the relative profitability of a given unit or function runs counter to the theme of collective responsibility as well as practical considerations of how actually to produce the relevant numbers. American or British institutions, however, where individual authority and responsibility characterise the management process, are much more receptive to such measurement.

Assuming a desire to measure performance, a critical variable is the organisational structure of an international function. To the extent that functional orientation plays a major role, as in the case of US banks utilising matrix management or Japanese and Continental European banks for whom 'international' itself is more a function than a geographic determination, it is relatively difficult to assign costs and revenues to a given unit or function. In a large US bank it is not easy to isolate the relative contribution made by the product expert and the geographic specialist who both collaborate on a specific transaction. On the other hand, if all of a given bank's activities are organised along geographic lines, profit allocation becomes a relatively simple affair of assigning costs and revenues to the geographic unit which performs the transaction.

A bank's management information system is obviously an important element in the measurement of performance. As their international operations evolve over a period of time, bankers have typically become aware of a number of shortcomings in their system. Firstly, they invariably must be modified to handle the volume and complexity of transactions carried on by the typical international bank. Such a modification probably involves moving from a manual to computer accounting system with all its attendant complications, and often an increase in computer capacity and sophistication at a later date. Secondly, information needed for management decisions may be produced in accounting formats which are not particularly relevant for such determinations as the relative profitability of a given customer relationship, service function or dealing room.

Finally, the absolute volume of reports generated tends to overwhelm management. It is standard bureaucratic practice for reports to be ordered by individual managers for their own purposes and for the preparation of these reports to continue well beyond their usefulness or even the retirement date of the individual who originally requested them. From time to time, therefore, major overhauls of the information system are undertaken to improve the quality and usefulness of reports and eliminate those no longer needed.

Responses to the questionnaire indicated a general satisfaction with the adequacy of a bank's management information system, with the qualification in almost all cases that some improvements would be useful. Two-thirds of the 35 banks responding to the question indicated such satisfaction. Those responding in the negative were less concerned about their ability to exercise control in risk sectors such as country limits and dealing positions, than they were about receiving data upon which intelligent management decisions on relative profitability or allocation of resources could be made. For example, all but 3 of 32 responding banks indicated that the basic information in Table 9.1 was received on a regular basis, and those few exceptions related to the profit contribution of individual operating units. While data other than that listed in Table 9.1 are certainly important in managing an international function, the Table should include the key elements required to manage the essential variables. The typical international bank manager, therefore, is concerned with improving his information flow to eliminate irrelevant reports, obtaining more timely information and receiving it in a form which facilitates decision-making.

TABLE 9.1. Standard management information received by international bank management

A. Do you feel you have adequate management information to run your international function?

B. Which of the following do you receive on a regular basis?
   - —total international profit contribution on a monthly or quarterly basis
   - —complete description of foreign exchange positions on a daily or weekly basis
   - —regular deposit mismatch reports showing liquidity as well as profit risk
   - —complete loan portfolio analysis including country exposure on a weekly or monthly basis
   - —profit centre analysis on a monthly or quarterly basis showing contribution of major departments and offshore entities
   - —regular reports on loans considered as bearing a risk of possible loss

Profit determination is a key element of all bank performance measurement systems. In this respect the framework in which profit is viewed is of great significance. In other words, having made the necessary arbitrary allocations of costs and revenues to obtain a 'bottom line' contribution of the international function to the bank as a whole, in what context is the absolute figure placed by senior bank management?

As pointed out in Chapter 7, 85 per cent of the sample banks interviewed have, in spite of the arbitrary allocations necessary, established a bottom line international contribution figure in which they have a certain amount of confidence. Such relative agreement, however, does not exist when the same bankers are asked how they or their senior management evaluate the bottom line contribution: in terms of return on capital, return on assets, percentage of total bank profits, or the absolute figure itself.

Of the 35 banks responding to the question, 15 or 43 per cent consider return on assets as the principal standard of measurement for an international department's contribution. Another 6, or 17 per cent use some combination of return on assets and return on capital, while an equivalent number take the absolute result itself as the ultimate criterion of performance. Return on capital and percentage of bank profits are each regarded by 4 banks as the applicable standard.

US and Canadian banks tend to show the greatest degree of unanimity in that all but 4 of the 21 responding place primary reliance on either return on assets, return on capital or a combination of the two. Most non-North American banks admit that bank-wide agreement on the appropriate standard of measurement does not exist either because of a lack of concern with profit measurement or the difficulty of reaching agreement on the proper approach. A large proportion of these bankers did not, therefore, feel they could respond to the question. In such a situation, the relative self-interest of the executive involved becomes apparent: the head of a rapidly expanding international function points with pride to his growing absolute earnings or increasing contribution to the total bank, while his superior or domestic equivalent focuses on that contribution in relation to capital or assets utilised by, or imputed to, the international function.

It is the procedure for imputing capital as well as loan loss reserve to the international function which causes the greatest amount of agony in the process of profit measurement and evaluation. While recognising from an intellectual standpoint that the international function uses an often substantial portion of the bank's capital funds, managers find it difficult to agree on exactly how capital and the loan loss reserve should be allocated. In the absence of such agreement, many senior bankers as a second best alternative simply calculate a raw return on international assets figure which does not take income from imputed capital into consideration. In similar vein, many European banks evaluate their own overseas units by entirely different standards: a capitalised subsidiary or affiliate is evaluated in terms of return on actual equity, while a branch's performance is looked at in terms of return on assets. Other banks, as mentioned previously, carefully allocate capital and loss reserves to individual categories of assets, on the basis of presumed levels of risk and global capitalisation factors which assume that the international function of the bank has the same cost of capital as the overall institution.

The relative focus of profit measurement in a given bank

effectively evolves along with the development of its international function. At the outset, absolute profit contribution or percentage of the total bank's earnings is usually the dominant consideration, but as the proportion of overall resources represented by international increases to, say, 20 per cent or more, there is a much greater incentive to evaluate the function in terms of such asset or capital allocation. At this point the traditional competition for resources between the domestic and international functions may crystallise with a statistical argument over the relative profitability of the two units, with each side utilising allocation of capital and other statistics which support its argument.

Regardless of the criterion selected or the level of sophistication utilised, most banks have articulated specific profit targets for their international function. These may be expressed in terms of return on assets (say, 1 per cent after tax on assets utilised), return on capital (say, the maintenance of the existing level of return on stockholders' funds) or percentage of group total (say, moving from the present 25 per cent to 35 per cent of total bank profit over a given period of time). The relative importance of criteria may change over a period of time as new constraints appear, for example the awareness of a shortage of capital may convert a bank from a focus on absolute profit to return on invested funds.

Of all the banks interviewed, the UK and American institutions showed by far the greatest awareness of and sensitivity to the restraint imposed on asset growth by a finite capital base. The sophistication of the US and UK stock markets, coupled with the emphasis placed on capital adequacy by the relevant regulatory authorities, have made American and British bankers acutely aware of the balance sheet limitations imposed by such external factors and the consequent priority to be placed on off-balance sheet income and maximising average loan spreads. Such restraints are much less significant in the case of Japanese and Continental European banks which are either government-owned or represent unquestioned pillars of the domestic financial system. In either case, the leverage exercised by regulatory or market forces tends to be diluted, with the result that the use of scarce resources is only one of a number of considerations borne in mind by those with ultimate responsibility for the performance of the banking system.

THE EVIDENCE OF PUBLISHED DATA

As in the case of the loan loss experience analysed in Chapter 7, relatively reliable data on the overall profitability of the international function are available only in the case of US banks, which for several years have broken out their international performance statistics. Table 9.2 represents a compilation of the international earnings contribution of 10 top American banks contrasted with the relative performance of the domestic side of the business.

TABLE 9.2. Earnings growth of major US banks, 1972–7 (as percentages)

	Compound annual growth 1972–7	Growth 1976–7
International earnings growth		
BankAmerica Corp.	27.7	0.4
Citicorp	23.2	6.8
Chase Manhattan Corp.	9.7	(2.4)
Manufacturers Hanover Corp.	29.3	9.1
J. P. Morgan & Co.	23.2	10.8
Bankers Trust NY	21.2	44.1
Chemical NY Corp.	38.9	13.7
First Chicago Corp.	22.6	47.5
Continental Illinois	13.0	(20.0)
Security Pacific	32.2	120.7
Total	22.8	8.0
Domestic earnings growth		
BankAmerica Corp.	11.7	29.0
Citicorp	(5.9)	(39.3)
Chase Manhattan Corp.	(9.5)	87.0
Manufacturers Hanover Corp.	4.9	11.6
J. P. Morgan & Co.	5.0	4.1
Bankers Trust NY	(20.7)	(45.8)
Chemical NY Corp.	1.5	13.9
First Chicago Corp.	4.7	13.9
Continental Illinois	13.0	18.8
Security Pacific	10.2	24.6
Total	4.4	10.9

Source: Salomon Brothers.

Table 9.2 reflects an extraordinary compound annual growth rate between 1972 and 1977 for the 10 banks of 22.8 per cent in contrast to one of 4.4 per cent per annum for domestic earnings. In 1977, however, international growth slowed to 8 per cent and was actually overtaken by a 10.9 per cent increase in domestic contribution.

From this relatively fragmentary data, a number of tentative conclusions can be drawn. First, it would appear that the period of sharp percentage international earnings gains is over for most mature international banks, as the relative increase in operating costs, coupled with a higher level of competition and penetration of individual markets, combine to slow down the rate of earnings growth. On the other hand, it can be safely assumed that significant rates of growth will be shown in the future by relative newcomers to the market which do not yet have the infrastructural cost burden, and have room within their portfolio limits for the more attractively priced assets.

Of the 29 banks in the interview sample prepared to project a rate of international earnings growth for the medium term, 21 or roughly three-quarters estimated one between 10 and 20 per cent per annum. There was no significant statistical difference between the rate projected by North American banks on the one hand and that of the other half of the sample. Among the positive factors cited by bankers in estimating future growth were the development of new markets and products, as well as the amortisation of the cost of entry into such markets through the opening of branches and the build-up of experienced staff. Negative factors included the current competitive pressure on gross margins, rising cost levels, and the presence of domestic business regarded by senior management as offering a more attractive risk/reward profile than overseas lending.

While available data on the international profits earned by national banks is thus limited to US institutions, some perception of the relative profitability of international banking can be obtained by reference to a broader sample of Euro-banks, or institutions carrying on a purely international activity in a financial centre such as London. Table 9.3 provides median and average return on capital and asset ratios in 1976 and 1977 for a sample of 46 such Euro-banks based in the UK.

Pure international banks in recent years have thus shown typical net earnings (after the 52 per cent UK corporate tax) of

TABLE 9.3 Return on Assets and Capital for 46 UK-based Euro-banks in 1976 and 1977

	1976		1977	
	Average	Median	Average	Median
Net profit as % of total assets	0.50	0.46	0.38	0.41
Net profit as % of stockholder funds	10.11	10.11	7.94	10.00

Source: IBCA Banking Analysis Ltd. (data taken from published annual statements)

roughly 0.40–0.50 per cent on total assets, and of approximately 8–10 per cent on stockholder funds. Such average results mask substantially better profits from institutions benefiting from stockholder-directed business, the ability to generate business and fees, or with particularly profitable specialities, while much poorer results have been shown by banks with loan loss problems, little fee income, or a minimum of direct customer business.

What is significant for the national banks which are the subject of this book is that such pure international institutions have produced results which are not significantly different from those of the domestic institutions which generally control these Euro-banks. Table 9.4 substantiates this point by providing average return on equity and total assets for a sample of national banks in the US, UK, West Germany, Canada, Holland, and France. The data are obviously of limited value because of national variations in accounting practice, relative importance of international earnings, nominal and effective tax rates and levels of leverage or gearing, but it is interesting to note that earnings on total assets, with the exception of the French sample, have been reasonably comparable with the 0.40–0.50 per cent earned on assets by the typical purely international bank. Net returns on stockholder funds, however, tend to be higher than in the case of the Euro-banks in large part because of the latters' lower gearing. It would appear, therefore, that a Euro-currency loan portfolio funded primarily from wholesale money market deposits can produce an unexciting but acceptable yield on capital funds and assets compared to domestic lending which may involve wider gross margins due in part to

TABLE 9.4 Comparative Profitability of Selected National Banking Institutions (years ending approx. 31 December, 1976 and 1977)

	1976		1977	
	Net income as % of average total assets	Net income as % of average stock-holder funds	Net income as % of average total assets	Net income as % of average stock-holder funds
United States average of 28 banks with over $5 billion in assets	0.54	11.13	0.53	11.58
United Kingdom average of 12 large commercial banks	0.52	10.99	0.59	12.08
West Germany average of 8 universal banks	0.35	10.76	0.37	10.78
Canada average of 4 large banks	0.65	16.61	0.58	15.69
Holland average of 4 large banks	0.45	13.90	0.45	14.02
France average of 5 large banks	0.24	12.51	0.22	10.69

Source: IBCA Banking Analysis Ltd. and Keefe, Bruyette & Woods, Inc.

cheaper deposits, but higher expense levels. More favourable loan loss experience internationally, with the exception of the institutions which have suffered primarily from property or shipping losses, has improved the picture for international lending, while the presence of significant fee and other non-interest differential earnings in some cases has produced returns on assets and capital which compare very favourably with domestic results. For those without the ability to generate a significant amount of business and the compensation which goes with this capability, however, the results of pure international banks tend to lag behind those of their domestic parents.

If one were to hazard a guess as to the profile of the international earnings of a typical national banking institution on the basis of the limited evidence available, the following tentative conclusions might be drawn.

Firstly, gross lending margins are in all likelihood narrower than those prevalent in most domestic markets. This phenomenon stems not only from the competitive tendency towards an international borrower's market which normally exists, but also from the relatively low portion of relatively cheap deposits in the typical international bank deposit mix.

This lower margin is partially offset at present by two factors. As pointed out previously, loan loss experience internationally has generally been a fraction of the domestic level for most banks around the world. Should banks' assumptions about the relative superiority of sovereign risk credit in this respect be borne out, this relatively favourable experience should continue. The other positive factor for many banks has been the relatively low level of operating costs necessary to support their international business when compared to the extensive and expensive branch network they must maintain domestically. Personnel and other costs associated with a high fixed asset base have thus been avoided by international functions, which can generate many times the gross earnings per employee or branch of a domestic function. As international networks expand, however, much of this cost advantage may be lost.

The only publicly available data comparing net interest margins on domestic and international loans are those given in the Annual Reports of major American banks. An analysis of the data between 1972 and 1977 of nine of the largest US banks shows that the differential between return on loans and cost of interest bearing deposits on international as opposed to the domestic equivalent shows no particular pattern.[1] In 1977, four of the nine showed such international margins significantly higher than their domestic equivalent. Trends for individual banks have varied significantly over time, as international margins will rise above domestic for a period of time or vice versa. Of the 53 possible occurrences (nine banks over six years), 28 or 53 per cent showed higher international margins. These figures, of course, do not allow for non-interest bearing deposits which would swing the balance significantly in favour of domestic margins.

In summary, therefore, one can tentatively conclude on the basis of experience to date that net international banking margins for the average institution are not significantly different from those of their domestic business, in large part because of the offsetting impact of various factors such as loss experience and cost of deposits. Enormous relative variations in such margins are experienced by different banks as a result of variances in type of business, network infrastructures, loan loss experience and other factors.

Ultimate success both domestically and overseas would, therefore, seem to be a function of such factors as a bank's ability to originate profitable transactions with customers, to minimise loan losses through diversification of risk and other measures, to develop relatively cheap sources of deposits and to limit the growth of expenses. In short, the keys to success in international business are not all that different from those which determine relative domestic profitability.

10 Outlook and Issues for the Future

After a decade of remarkable growth and development beginning in the late 1960s, international banking in its post-World War II configuration has reached a certain level of maturity in its evolution. The unprecedented entry of newcomers into the Euro-currency market, the remarkable proliferation of their networks and the resulting fierce struggle for what is viewed as attractive business have brought the risk/reward ratio of traditional lending business, for the second time in five years, to levels which are unacceptable to a growing number of banks concerned with return on assets and capital. Pious principles about risk and reward uttered after the crises of confidence in 1970 and 1974 have once again been overwhelmed by the imperatives of planned profit targets, the perceived need to develop and maintain customer relationships, and the understandable human desire to do business even at marginal returns once an international infrastructure has been set up. Bankers who have now seen two full cycles of international banking behaviour have come to recognise, particularly with the added capacity introduced since the current cycle began in late 1974/early 1975, that the equilibrium tendency in international banking is movement towards a borrower's market characterised by serious structural overcapacity.

HOW BANKERS PERCEIVE THE FUTURE

In the competitive environment which existed in mid-1978, 40 senior bankers were asked to rank what they regarded as the most serious long-term threats to their international business. It is inevitable that responses to such questions at this point in time will reflect to a large extent immediate concerns. By focusing on a longer time frame and discussing responses in detail, however, it is possible to draw some useful tentative conclusions for the future behaviour of international bankers. This chapter will, therefore, summarise the responses of bankers to this question and subsequently describe some likely patterns of future management practices as well as issues which will preoccupy management over the next few years.

The greatest preoccupation of the 29 senior bankers responding to the question was, not surprisingly, competition and its impact on gross margins. This was cited by 10, or one-third, as their single greatest concern for the long term. North American bankers were particularly concerned about competition; roughly half of the 15 US and Canadians as against only 3, or 21 per cent of the 14 other bankers gave top priority to this preoccupation. Such a split in attitudes is reflected in current market trends where Japanese and European banks seem to be playing a relatively more aggressive role in syndicated credits at the expense of US institutions concerned with the trend in loan pricing.

Somewhat more surprising is the emphasis placed by many banks on human resources ('shortage of trained and capable staff') which was ranked as their primary concern by the next largest number of bankers—9, or 31 per cent of the total. More non-North American banks (5 out of 14) are thus concerned about people than competition (3) or loan losses (3). Given the somewhat late arrival on the international scene of many such banks and their relative shortage of corporate credit and other international banking skills, such an emphasis on qualified staff is quite understandable.

A distant third on the list of top bankerly worries is loan losses—from developing countries or any other type of customer. Only 3 of the 29 thus gave top priority to such losses; none of these was a North American banker. Most bankers interviewed expressed their firm conviction that the relatively good payments record of sovereign and bank borrowers would continue and that their loan loss performance would remain more favourable than that of their domestic colleagues.

A marginally different result is shown by analysing the three most serious threats cited by each of the bankers, many of whom were not prepared to cite one specific concern but preferred to list several of roughly equal importance. On this basis, competition once again was the most frequently mentioned problem: 28

bankers, including 18 North American and 10 others, cited it as one of their three major concerns. A total of 23 bankers, however, mentioned rising expense levels as a major problem. Interestingly enough, 16 of these bankers were US or Canadian as against only 7 from other parts of the world.

The third most frequently mentioned problem on this basis was the shortage of qualified people: 20 bankers, of which 11 were non-North American and 9 US or Canadian, expressed this concern. The fourth-ranked problem was possible losses from less-developed countries, which was a major concern to 10 bankers (4 North American and 6 others). Not surprisingly, bankers were usually quick to distinguish the quality of *their* particular sovereign risk portfolio from that of 'other banks'!

Other potential problems seemed to be of relatively little concern to the bankers interviewed. Five gave high ranking to the problem posed by a world-wide depression or political cataclysm and four were concerned about losses not related to developing countries. While a few voiced concern about another Herstatt-type crisis of confidence, most felt that the system could cope at least as well as it did in 1974 with such a problem. Several bankers were frank to admit that the greatest practical threat to their international business was the relative attractiveness of domestic business in their bank and their resulting inability to do business and therefore retain good people, clients and the infrastructure necessary to re-enter the international market at a future point in time.

From this questionnaire there thus emerges a picture of global concern with the obvious short and long-term problem of competition but also an almost equal preoccupation with expense levels and the shortage of qualified people. US banks, with their concern for return on assets and awareness of the scarcity of capital, are particularly worried about competition and its impact on lending margins. A number of banks throughout the world are quite bitter about the cyclical or periodic surge of lending interest on the part of banks which have not been consistent participants in the market, and the permanent damage to the viability of the market they feel such sporadic competition might cause. Almost equally important to American institutions, however, is the rising cost of overseas networks and other expense categories which become more visible and painful as gross margins decline.

European and Japanese banks, however, do not share the same concern for scarcity of capital funds and, therefore, are somewhat less agitated by competitive pressures. Their principal preoccupation is shortage of qualified people—credit, marketing staff and senior management—to cope with the aggressive expansion programmes on which they have embarked. While American and Canadian banks are aware of their human resource constraints, a number of the more mature institutions are trying to cope with almost the opposite problem—that of placing returning expatriate officers in home office jobs which they will regard as sufficiently challenging in comparison with their experience abroad.

POSSIBLE FUTURE PATTERNS OF BEHAVIOUR

The problem areas for the future are thus well defined both by these responses and by observation of actual market behaviour. The balance of this chapter will discuss how international bankers may try to resolve their problems and what issues are posed for the future by their efforts.

The problem of competition and its impact on gross margins is a major challenge not only in the fiercely competitive market of 1978, but also over the foreseeable future. Even if lending margins improve significantly above these levels, observers who have followed the 1974–8 cycle generally recognise that the substantial increase in capacity in the market since 1974 will further reinforce what appears to be a natural tendency towards a borrower's market in the Euro-currency sector.

Given such likely market conditions, what type of management responses are likely in the future? Some banks will undoubtedly drop out of the mainstream activity of Euro-currency lending and either put their international lending function on a 'care and maintenance' basis or divert resources to non-lending or non-international activities. The substantial reduction in lending activity by US regional banks in 1978 represents such a response. In so doing, management hopes that the risk/reward relationship of international as opposed to domestic lending will swing back in the former's favour within a reasonable period of time. If this is not the case, of course, the expense of maintaining a relatively inactive home office staff and overseas network can become difficult to justify, and the impact on morale may be such that key officers may choose to leave the international function rather than sit on their hands. Bankers may be encouraged in their patience by the rapid turnaround in 1974 from a borrower's to a lender's market following the Herstatt collapse. To withdraw even partially from Euro-currency lending in the knowledge that customer relationships may be impaired and the bank accused of being a 'fair weather lender', however, is an agonising decision for a bank's management.

Recognising that competition has been reflected primarily in lending margins, many banks are responding by emphasising non-lending activities in an effort to partially offset the competitive damage to their principal source of income. Fee earnings from the syndication of Euro-currency loans, Euro-bonds and other investment banking-type services; foreign exchange dealing; portfolio management services; a greater focus on the increased yield from intelligently mismatching global assets and liabilities; traditional banking services such as clearing accounts and trade finance, and non-banking activities such as leasing and specialist consulting are some of the non-lending activities which do not necessarily inflate the balance sheet but do provide extra revenue. For institutions such as the US and British banks without real experience in universal banking and existing investment banking relationships however, it must be acknowledged that an uphill fight will be necessary to significantly penetrate this market. While emphasis on the more traditional commercial banking services may bear fruit, the number of competitors with the same objectives in mind must necessarily limit opportunities in this sector.

Another response to competitive pressures is greater product differentiation along with a more articulated definition of a bank's identity and market strategy. One of the dominant impressions gained from the interviews conducted with senior bankers is the lack in most banks of a precise definition of marketing strategy, the image the bank wants to present to the market and the relatively unique products and markets it will emphasise. While a number of banks do have well articulated plans along these lines, most express their strategy in terms of generalisations with regard to quality of service and a number of traditional specialities stemming from domestic strengths, knowledge of certain geographic or functional areas and experience in trade finance. Although such expertise, service and products may be quite superior to those of the competition, when expressed by the typical calling officer to a potential client it may sound suspiciously like the expertise and service offered by a dozen other institutions. Most banks do try to pinpoint geographic and functional market opportunities where their particular strengths can produce relatively attractive results; the problem is usually to sufficiently differentiate in the customer's view the particular products and services offered from those made available by the competition and to relate them to the customer's specific needs.

A key element of such efforts to establish a market identity is the development of new products or services. Most bankers recognise that they are unlikely to be able to offer a truly unique product in such a highly competitive market with little product differentiation; their focus is, therefore, on providing generally accepted services with an emphasis on quality or professionalism. For these banks, so-called 'new product development' is the elaboration of services or products which may be new to that particular bank but hardly novel in the marketplace. A few others, however, make a genuine effort to develop and market unique services. On the other hand, a very large number of smaller and medium-sized banks feel they do not have the human and other resources to develop any new specialities and must, therefore, rely on whatever skills they presently have.

One future trend, therefore, will be the efforts by international banks to better define their strategy and market focus. Given the competitive constraints and traditional approach taken by most bankers, however, what is likely to emerge in most cases is a sharpened focus on existing strengths and a development of more traditional banking services rather than totally new products. Basic strategy will continue to be defined largely in terms of existing domestic strengths, both geographic and functional, and the exploitation of these natural advantages.

Another product of the priority placed on establishing a definable market identity and image—as well as to improve a network's responsiveness—will be a continuation of the recent trend away from consortia and joint ventures. While a few such organisations will be set up *de novo* to exploit fairly specific, well-defined market opportunities, a more powerful trend will be the weakening of co-operation among partners of existing multi-bank ventures and the actual dissolution or restructuring of several of them.

The problem of rising expense levels poses one of the major issues for international bankers. One of the historical attractions of international lending for national banks has been the relatively low cost of building a given revenue base as opposed to that which supports their domestic business. In its simplest form, an international function can generate a loan portfolio of hundreds of millions of dollars equivalent using a handful of people in head office, simply by responding to telex offers of loan participations and making a limited number of new business calls. As the home office line and staff functions are built up and an overseas network put in place, however, such functions become exposed to the same inflationary currents and increase in non-revenue-producing staff which have afflicted their domestic counterparts. International banks are thus confronted with the conflict between, on the one hand, the demands for greater sophistication of staff and systems, and, on the other, the sharply rising costs, in an inflationary world, of achieving these objectives.

The priority placed by American banks on controlling expenses is a product not only of their particular sensitivity to profitability considerations, but also of the relative maturity of their home office and network infrastructure. It is, therefore, a reasonable assumption that other banks will feel the same pressures as they follow the development pattern established by American and other banks with a relatively mature international business.

Actions taken by international banks to limit expense growth will clearly vary significantly from bank to bank. As indicated in Chapter 8, American banks are quite disposed to closing down offices and branches if the quantifiable contribution to the bank as a whole is clearly unsatisfactory, while non-US institutions are more prepared to live with such loss-making operations. Whether or not offices are actually closed, however, a greater focus on cost effectiveness will imply a more rigorous financial analysis of proposed offices, the willingness to cut out relatively unprofitable activities in some existing units, attempts to computerise or take other steps to limit the increase in administrative staff, and a more critical approach taken to controllable expenses such as travel, entertainment, advertising and promotion. In home office, across-the-board salary increases may be viewed with less liberality, while attempts will be made to reduce the cost of expatriate personnel through the greater use of local staff. Many international staff functions such as tax, personnel and audit may be combined with the respective domestic department to reduce overall costs, and even line functions such as corporate lending or money dealing may thus be merged to achieve economies. Greater attention will be paid to account profitability, and relationships which are deemed to be unprofitable will be charged accordingly or encouraged to leave the bank.

A greater stress on the recruiting, training and career development of qualified staff will constitute a major trend in international banking. In this, as in other problem areas, the lead offered by American banks will probably be followed by other institutions. These latter often have the disadvantage, vis-à-vis American banks, of having to develop linguistic as well as corporate credit, marketing and management skills, whereas the US banks had a natural head start in many of these areas.

Faced with the need to build skill levels in so many areas of activity, most banks will abandon traditional recruiting and training structures which resulted in the hiring of a mass of relatively young recruits, regardless of educational level, and channelling these individuals through a standard bottom-up training programme with little early recognition of those specially qualified for international or senior management positions. Greater emphasis will probably be placed on hiring high-potential university and business school graduates, and these individuals will be given an increasingly specialised training programme focusing on the skills associated with the international function. In-house training programmes to upgrade the skills of existing personnel and training periods outside the bank at universities and other banks will become more common. Transfers of high-potential domestic officers to the international function will become more frequent, although language barriers and internal resistance to such transfers will pose some limitations.

Equally important will be a growing degree of executive mobility as banks find that the necessary skills can be acquired most easily by recruitment from other institutions. While the resulting influx of new personnel and new ideas will cause problems in the more traditional structures, it will usually be perceived as a better alternative than transferring domestic officers who may not have the linguistic or other skills necessary in international banking. Non-American banks will probably hire back from US institutions many of their nationals, who had joined the latter many years previously to free themselves from the traditional constraints of their national institutions.

SOME UNRESOLVED ISSUES

For all of these changes in skill levels and executive mobility, international banks will continue to be managed primarily by bankers who have proven themselves in a particular aspect of the banking business. As a result their management approach will reflect some of the weaknesses of bankers as managers described earlier in the book: a relative unfamiliarity with and lack of commitment to marketing and product development; a similar lack of commitment to strategic planning and a relative unwillingness to move people and change structures if performance does not measure up; and an unwillingness to recognise risk as a legitimate strategic variable. This is not to say that international banks can or should be run by managers from the automobile or chemical industries, but simply that bank management will continue to be a distinctive phenomenon with its own particular strengths and weaknesses. In the future, therefore, one can anticipate that the herd instinct which has characterised so much international banking behaviour is unlikely to change significantly. New products and banking techniques will certainly be developed, but it is unrealistic to expect a much greater degree of product differentiation among banks, who will continue to rely primarily on traditional relationships, as well as their established services and areas of specialisation, to compete in the marketplace.

Another issue which will preoccupy international bank management in the future is that of the appropriate orientation towards customers and the resulting impact on organisational forms and patterns of behaviour. As the customer marketing survey discussed in chapter 6 made clear, international banks in general are widely criticised for a lack of understanding of their current and prospective customer base and frequent failures in responding to and assisting in the solution of customers' problems. While only a limited number of banks have actually surveyed customers and prospects to evaluate these criticisms, a number have taken action to deal with the problems of customer interface and service by bringing to bear a higher and broader level of expertise and improving decision-making procedures.

In organisations such as US banks with a primarily geographic orientation, the traditional split between international and domestic customer responsibility constitutes a major obstacle to effectively responding to a customer request for truly global service. To overcome the problems of internal conflicts and variable levels of expertise which this poses, banks have and will continue to adopt a variety of courses of action. At one extreme is the naming of a global account officer from either the domestic or international function for local or possibly foreign-based multinationals, who calls upon other functions in the bank for assistance in servicing the relationship. This may be coupled with the delineation within the international function of a service group which provides staff support on international business to line account officers in the domestic banking department. At the other extreme are a number of US banks which have completely eliminated the geographic factor in assigning account responsibility by either creating a separate multinational line department to handle customers with international needs, or moving to a full matrix structure where the traditional geographic breakdown is fully matched by a functional organisation, so that at least two individuals are generally involved in the solution of a particular customer problem.

The resulting modification of organisational structures in a bank with a traditional geographic orientation obviously creates internal stresses and tensions in addition to at least temporarily disrupting the existing relationship with the customer as new individuals and procedures are introduced. Whether this overall disruption is a lesser evil than the previous problem of co-ordination across organisational lines is a matter of great debate among American banks; suffice it to say that many institutions will continue to modify their customer interface in the future without necessarily finding a totally satisfactory solution. The difficulty in resolving this problem is, of course, largely a function of the sheer physical size of many banks who will find it difficult to respond to client needs whatever organisational format is used.

Organisational change, albeit to a lesser extent, is also likely in non-North American banks organised primarily on a functional basis which are reinforcing the credit and marketing strengths of their international department to serve their multinational customers better. In such cases, resistance to organisational change may be stronger than in US institutions, while the difficulty of building a competent, multilingual and experienced staff may well be greater than in a North American bank. As a result of these trends, one can envisage North American and British banks moving towards the Japanese and European-style functional approach with an integrated orientation towards customers, while, conversely, the latter banks move in the direction of American-style geographic focus with relatively self-standing international functions. In all of these moves to better service customers with international interests, the likely outcome will be influenced to a significant extent by the relative influence and preference of a few key individuals in the organisation, in view of the impact of this change on their individual positions in the organisation.

Along with organisational change may well come greater efforts to determine the requirements of corporate customers and take the necessary action to modify marketing strategies. American banks in recent years have come to rely to a greater extent on in-depth interviews with customers and prospects to replace the superficial generalisations about customer objectives which have traditionally characterised bank business development strategies. An increasing number of other banks may also take such samplings. It is unlikely, however, that marketing as a management practice will penetrate bankers' thinking to the extent that it has outside banking, because of the traditional reluctance of bankers to envisage themselves as salesmen marketing products. Marketing experts from outside banking may be hired or internal marketing functions established, but the impact on actual behaviour is not likely to be significant.

The long-term trend of international loan losses is an issue which will continue to preoccupy bankers. Unkind critics often express the view that bankers can hardly be expected to regard their loan loss outlook with anything but the relative optimism expressed in the responses to the questionnaire. The historical record of international lending since World War II certainly supports this optimism, and the relative rate of return calculations made by most international bankers reflect a continuation of loss experience far more favourable than that of their domestic business. However, the jury is still out, both on the question of sovereign risk loan losses and of individual banks' ability to manage their sovereign exposure, and significant losses on either sovereign risk or private sector loans could wreck the international strategy of many institutions. International loan pricing with its relatively low gross margins has implicitly assumed correspondingly low loss experience.

Perhaps the greatest danger here is the temptation during periods of intense competition to reach for truly marginal public and private sector credits which alone seem to offer an acceptable yield. The tendency to maintain at least a minimal level of lending activity during such periods is a strong one, particularly among banks who have recently geared up an extensive infrastructure to participate in the market.

A totally different concern stems from the importance of bankers' confidence in sovereign risk lending: an increasing number of such borrowers are in the hands of their private sector bankers not only to roll over existing foreign debt but also to lend net new money.

A loss of confidence on the part of even a few major lenders can spread rapidly to other banks, each of which makes its own lending decisions, with the result that it may become impossible to organise a necessary refinancing. Whether or not there is a justified credit concern, therefore, the net result is an effective freezing of all banks' exposure to that particular borrower, with the prospect of a long and agonising process of negotiations involving up to several hundred bankers and several dozen different syndicates. Actual losses in the form of write-offs of sovereign risk loans may be only a minor concern to bankers and regulatory authorities in comparison with the percentage of outstandings to countries which, for practical purposes, are unable to refinance without such negotiations.

These actual or potential losses must be regarded in the particular context in which non-bankers perceive international loans. US banks in the mid-1970s have seen the suspicion and concern with which the investment fraternity, Boards of Directors, legislative authorities, news media and others view the risk in international lending as compared to domestic business. Whether it is because of the exotic and often ill-understood nature of international lending or a subjective view that banks should concentrate their efforts domestically, a given loss abroad has had a greater impact in the US on the perceptions of such influential outside constituencies than an equivalent loss to a local company. In this context, bankers must consider the ramifications of even a relatively small international loan problem on their stock market rating, the legislative and regulatory climate, and the attitude of Boards of Directors, to the future of their international business as a whole. Another unresolved issue for the entire international banking sector is the absence of a lender of last resort in a rapidly growing market characterised by periodic bouts of extreme nervousness and loss of confidence. While the 1974 confidence crisis was resolved with minimal long-run damage to the banking community, there is nothing to prevent a repetition of a Herstatt-type crisis, and the central banks which could supply a safety net in such an event are unlikely to do so except on an *ad hoc* basis when the next crisis occurs. International bankers must, therefore, do their planning with this continued uncertainty in mind.

An issue raised by Nigel Hudson's volume, the *Money Dealing Function In International Banking*, is the vulnerability of international banks to dealing room losses through mechanical errors, bad judgement, or unauthorised dealing in an environment characterised by extremely high volumes of transactions and a large network of dealing functions throughout the world. Even the most sophisticated control systems cannot completely eliminate such possibilities, so that once again international bank management must reckon with a major imponderable.

THE CENTRAL IMPORTANCE OF PROFITABILITY

How all of these issues are resolved will ultimately determine the outcome of what most bankers regard as the central problem of international profitability. As mentioned above, international banking can be regarded as a mature industry with a considerable degree of over-capacity. It is difficult to find historical parallels for a competitive environment where hundreds of institutions operating around the world sell roughly the same services at roughly the same price through thousands of profit-oriented units to a group of clients whose relative desirability is a subject of almost universal agreement. In such an environment, it is not surprising that, apart from the occasional crisis of confidence, as in 1974, conditions tend to approximate more often than not to those of the economists' definition of pure competition.

One of the contributory factors to this state of affairs is the difference in views as to how profits should be measured. Banks which do not have significant capital constraints or whose international exposure is relatively low tend to evaluate profits in absolute terms or as a percentage of total earnings, while those concerned about limited resources and conscious of more attractive lending opportunities focus on return on capital or assets. The former institutions—at least for a certain period of time—are, therefore, prepared to accept a lower level of compensation for a given risk as long as absolute profit growth is satisfactory, an attitude which obviously undermines the entire pricing structure.

While the international banking market should continue to grow in aggregate terms because of its clear attraction to borrowers and depositors alike, the aggregate rate of profit growth is unlikely to keep step, as a result of competitive pressures and the steady rise in costs. As in the past, individual banks will enter the international market, build a certain level of infrastructure and absolute profits, and then show a relative decline in the rate of international earnings growth as its level of non-interest expenses rises and external constraints such as more attractive domestic opportunities or capital limitations become significant. Faced with a major deterioration in their risk/reward configuration for international lending, many banks will opt out of interest differential lending and turn to domestic banking or off-balance sheet and fee earning activities to pick up the slack. As discussed above, major efforts will be made by the more pragmatic institutions to cut back expense levels.

Timing will continue to be a key variable in an individual bank's profit picture. Those courageous or fortunate enough to add significantly to their loan book at a time of high spreads such as 1975 are likely to show better results than banks who build their portfolio in periods such as 1978, and who may in addition pick up a few bad loans in their eagerness to do business. The prepayment phenomenon will reduce but not eliminate such an advantage. A number of American and other banks over the past decade have deliberately moved resources from domestic to international and back again to offset losses or poor growth in one marketplace.

All international bankers will be subject to unfavourable factors beyond their individual ability to control: competition, crises of confidence, world economic and political conditions and so forth. Where individual banks will distinguish themselves will be in the sectors over which management can exercise some control: the attracting and development of superior personnel with a level of expertise respected by customers; an articulated marketing strategy that successfully differentiates its product line; the restraint of non-interest expense growth and development of a cost-effective overseas network; and the maintenance of a loss ratio consistent with the level of gross margin received.

It must be admitted, however, that the majority of international banks will continue as in the past to move with the tide of their peer group and be guided by the management traditions of the past. The limited amount of available data indicates that international banking profitability has not been significantly different from that of the domestic markets in which most national banks operate. In the future, however, the external and internal forces described above will force banks either to accept an unattractive level of profitability, leave the market or utilise their management strengths to demonstrate superior performance. Those banks prepared to innovate and move away from the herd on such issues as management development, control of costs and product development are likely to be among the latter.

Appendix A: 40 Banks composing Interview Sample

Algemene Bank Nederland NV
Bank of America
American Security and Trust Company NA
Australia and New Zealand Banking Group Ltd.
Banca Nazionale dell'Agricoltura
Banca Nazionale del Lavoro
Banco Hispano Americano
Banque l'Indochine et de Suez
Banque Nationale de Paris
Banque Worms
Canadian Imperial Bank of Commerce
Citibank NA
Continental Illinois National Bank and Trust Company of Chicago
Credito Italiano
Crocker National Bank
Dai-Ichi Kangyo Bank Ltd
Dresdner Bank AG
The Fidelity Bank
First City National Bank of Houston
The First National Bank of Chicago
Girard Trust Bank
Harris Trust and Savings Bank
Hessische Landesbank-Girozentrale
Hong Kong and Shanghai Banking Corporation
Lloyds Bank Ltd
Morgan Guaranty Trust Company of New York
National City Bank (Cleveland)
National Westminster Bank Ltd
The Bank of Nova Scotia
The Philadelphia National Bank
Rainier National Bank

Security Pacific National Bank
Société Générale de Belgique
Swiss Bank Corporation
Texas Commerce Bank NA
The Toronto-Dominion Bank
The Bank of Tokyo Ltd
Union Bank of Switzerland
Union Commerce Bank
United California Bank

Appendix B: Questionnaire Submitted to 40 Banks

1. How would you rank the following objectives of your international banking function in terms of importance?

   (a) net profit contribution to the bank
   (b) service existing customers of the bank
   (c) meet the competition of other banks
   (d) develop new business/customers for your bank
   (e) other objectives

2. Which of the following best describes the organisational structure in your international function:

   A. *Decision-making*

   (i) decentralised decision-making with significant use of regional headquarters and delegation to officers in the field, or
   (ii) centralised structure with home office making the bulk of the credit and other decisions

   B. *Marketing*

   (i) functional/product related approach to customers with emphasis on industry or functional specialisation, or
   (ii) geographic approach with focus on regional expertise.

   C. *Interaction with Domestic Banking Function*

(i) is there a so-called 'multinational' or 'world corporation' group which has line marketing responsibility for major corporations throughout the world with cross-border operations and, there-

fore, cuts across the traditional 'domestic vs. international' distinction?
(ii) is there a single head of international banking with no other major responsibilities?
(iii) if so, to whom does he report?
(iv) would it be possible to have a copy of your international organisation chart?

3. The Credit Function

A. *Decision-making Process*

Would you say that you rely more heavily for credit decisions on:
(i) a credit committee which vets most credit proposals, or
(ii) credit limits to individual bank officers who are able to commit to most loans without reference to a committee.

B. Which of the following levels of loan loss reserve (as a percent of outstandings) do you feel would be most appropriate *in the future* for your international business:

0.0% to 0.5%
0.5% to 1.0%
1.0% to 1.5%
1.5% or higher

4. Profitability

A. Do you calculate an estimated profit contribution of your international function to your bank? If so, is it

0–10% of the total
10–20%
20–30%
30–40%
40–50%
50% or more?

B. Do you expect this percentatage contribution to increase in the medium term?

C. Does your bank feel there is a policy limit to the percentage which international should represent as a portion of the total?

D. Which of the following profitability criteria do you consider most relevant to your international business?

return on assets employed
return on capital (imputed if necessary) utilised
percentage of overall bank profits
absolute level of profits
another criterion?

E. What rate of profit growth do you consider most likely over the medium term for your international business?

5. Competitive Strategy

How would you rank the following competitive strategies in terms of importance to your international function?

provide specialist expertise in specific sectors which cannot be surpassed
offering unique products and services
ability to commit large amounts of financing
speed and flexibility of decision-making
large, loyal customer base coupled with knowledge of their requirements
ability to quote the finest/best terms
geographic coverage of the market
other factor?

6. Range of Products/Diversification

Do you regard it as important to offer a range of services going beyond the traditional deposit/lending and trade financing services traditionally provided by international commercial banks?

If so, which of the following do you consider important to your international strategy?

merchant/investment banking
leasing, factoring and other bank related services
non-finance related activities such as consulting, equity investments, etc.

7. Future Outlook

   How would you rank the following in terms of seriousness of threat to your international business in the long run?

   credit losses from heavily-borrowed developing countries
   other credit losses
   competition and its impact on gross profits
   rising expense levels
   shortage of trained, competent people
   a world depression or political cataclysm which is effectively beyond the power of individual bankers to prevent
   a crisis of banking confidence such as Herstatt which becomes a self-fulfilling prophecy
   another problem?

8. Staffing:

   (a) what was the age of the present head of international when he assumed this job?
   (b) how many years had he been with the bank before assuming this function?
   (c) did the bank's present chief executive pass through the international function as part of his career path?
   (d) does the present head of international have a university degree?
   (e) how many employees are there in the international function?
   (f) can you estimate the amount of international profits per international employee?
   (g) does the international department have its own specific training programme for university graduates?

9. Overseas Network:

   A. Which of the following best describes your strategy in establishing an overseas banking network?

   offices/branches which do extensive local as well as international business in a large number of national markets abroad offices/branches in most or all of the world's leading financial centres which primarily carry on international business

offices/branches only in a limited number of offshore centres so as to permit home office access to the international market

no offshore offices beyond a limited number of representatives who do not do business directly

B. Would you say that your overseas network is

largely in place (based on present market circumstances)

a significant expansion still to occur

at the beginning of a major expansion phase.

C. Which of the following best describes your attitude to consortium/joint venture operations?

would never consider them

only if it is the only way to penetrate a given market

very useful and appropriate for your organisation

D. Which of the following best describes your attitude to the profitability of a given offshore entity?

profits are attributed to each offshore office/implantation and the office is closed/merged with another if a minimum profit contribution is not achieved

we try to measure the profit contribution of most or all of the entities but would place a high value on non-financial considerations in opening or closing an office

profitability of individual offices is not of major importance in evaluating individual parts of the network

10. Management Information:

A. Do you feel you have adequate management information to run your international function?

B. Which of the following do you receive on a regular basis?

total international profit contribution on a monthly or quarterly basis complete description of F/X positions on a daily or weekly basis

regular deposit mismatch reports showing liquidity as well as profit risk

complete loan portfolio analysis including country exposure on a weekly or monthly basis

profit centre analysis on a monthly or quarterly basis showing contribution of major departments and offshore entities

regular reports on loans considered as bearing a risk of possible loss

Appendix C: Questionnaire Submitted to 30 Senior Corporate Financial Officers

1. *Selection of International Banks*

    A. Are there any circumstances under which you would add to the list of banks presently providing international services to you? Do you actually discourage 'cold calls' by banks which have no present relationship with you?

    B. If you are prepared to add to your list of banks, could you list, in order of importance, the criteria on which such a bank would be selected?

        willingness to assume credit risk (such as country credit) others not prepared to take
        fineness of their terms (spread, maturity, etc.)
        personal relationships which facilitate doing business together
        new or imaginative solution to a problem
        speed and responsiveness of decision-making process
        size of the commitment they can make
        comprehensive range of services
        another criterion?

2. *Evaluation of Banks' Marketing Approach*

    A. If you were to criticise the efforts by international banks to develop a relationship with your company, which of the following possible criticisms would be the most relevant?

        lack of preparation/understanding of your business
        lack of any specific product/solution to propose

inability to commit to a specific proposal without time-consuming reference to home office
inability to meet competitive terms
another criticism

B. When you suggest a specific set of terms/credit risk to a prospective banker to initiate a relationship and he agrees to go beyond the terms offered by your existing bankers, does this create a positive or negative impression as to the new bank's professionalism?

3. *Evaluation of Present Banking Relationships*

In what order of priority do you rank the following criteria in terms of evaluating the usefulness of an existing international banking relationship?

understanding of your business as reflected in the flexibility/intelligence of the banker's response to your problems
fineness of terms (pricing, maturity, security, etc.)
comprehensive range of services and size of network
speed and responsiveness of decision-making process
imagination in suggesting solutions to problems
ability to meet your financial requirements from its own resources
another criterion?

4. *General Comments*

Would you care to make any general comments on international banks and bankers which you think would be relevant to their efforts to develop business with your firm?

Notes

NOTES TO CHAPTER 1

1. Steven I. Davis, *The Euro-Bank: its Origins, Management and Outlook.*
2. Among them are F. John Mathis (ed.), *Offshore Lending by US Commercial Banks,* and D. R. Mandich *et al* (eds.), *Foreign Exchange Trading Techniques and Controls.*
3. The reader is referred to Geoffrey Bell, *The Euro-Dollar Market and the International Financial Systems,* and Brian Scott Quinn, *The New Euromarkets* (1975).

NOTES TO CHAPTER 2

1. Raymond de Roover, *The Rise and Decline of the Medici Bank, 1397–1494.*
2. Ibid.
3. Richard Kaeuper, *Bankers to the Crown: The Riccardi of Lucca in the Service of Edward I,* p. 83.
4. Richard Ehrenberg, *Capital and Finance in the Age of the Renaissance* (1928).
5. Kaeuper, op. cit., p. 249.
6. de Roover, op. cit. p. 5.
7. Ibid, p. 372.
8. David Joslin, *A Century of Banking in Latin America*: Ch. 13: Bank of London and South America, pp. 234–53.
9. Maurice Collis, *Wayfoong: The Hong Kong and Shanghai Banking Corporation,* p. 33.
10. Ibid, p. 67.
11. Geoffrey Tyson, *100 Years of Banking in Asia and Africa, 1863–1963 (A History of National and Grindlays Bank Limited),* p. 68.
12. J. A. Henry, *The First Hundred Years of the Standard Bank.*
13. The Mitsui Bank Ltd, *A History of the First Hundred Years.*
14. Fritz Seidenzahl, *1870–1970: 100 Jahre Deutsche Bank.*
15. Société Générale, *Société Générale de Belgique: 1822–1972.*
16. A. J. S. Baster, *The International Banks.*
17. Ralph W. Hidy, *The House of Baring in American Trade and Finance,* p. 419.
18. Marten G. Buist, *At Spes Non Fracta: Hope & Co.: 1770–1817,* p. 27.
19. Leland H. Jenks, *Migration of British Capital to 1875,* p. 282.

20. Rondo Cameron, 'The Crédit Mobilier and the Economic Development of Europe'.
21. A. J. S. Baster, op. cit.
22. Ibid., p. 40.
23. Clyde Phelps, *The Foreign Expansion of American Banks.*
24. Ibid., pp. 164–5.
25. Hal B. Lary, *The United States in the World Economy*, p. 118.
26. T. W. Lamont as quoted in Siegfried Stern, *The United States in International Banking.*
27. Siegfried Stern, p. 212.
28. Otto Kahn as quoted in Stern, p. 217.

NOTES TO CHAPTER 3

1. See Ehrenberg (op. cit.) for discussion of Lyon and Antwerp markets in 16th Century.
2. Federal Reserve Board press release (June 1978).
3. Ursel Steuber, *International Banking: The Foreign Activities of the Banks of Principal Industrial Countries*, p. 10.
4. Deutsche Bundesbank monthly reports.
5. Federal Reserve Board, *US Offices of Foreign Banks: The Recent Experience* (private circulation, 1978).
6. Bank of England monthly bulletins.

NOTES TO CHAPTER 4

1. For an excellent detailed analysis of a US bank's motives for expanding internationally and selecting the vehicles through which it will expand, the reader is referred to Francis A. Lees, *International Banking and Finance.*
2. Cary Reich, 'America's new generation of International Bankers', p. 37.
3. Ibid., p. 38.

NOTES TO CHAPTER 9

1. T. H. Donaldson, *International Lending by Commercial Banks*, Chapter 9.

Bibliography

Baker, James C. and Bradford, M. Gerald, *American Banks Abroad: Edge Act Companies and Multinational Banking* (London: Praeger, 1974).

Bank for International Settlements, *Annual Reports.*

Bank of England, *Quarterly Bulletin.*

Baster, A. J. S. *The International Banks* (London: King, 1935).

Bell, Geoffrey, *The Euro-dollar Market and the International Financial System* (London: Macmillan, 1973).

Bennett, Edward W. *Germany and the Diplomacy of the Financial Crisis, 1931* (Cambridge, Mass: Harvard University Press, 1962).

Blunden, George, 'The Supervision of the UK Banking System', *Bank of England Quarterly Bulletin,* 15 (1975) 188–94.

Brimmer, Andrew F. 'American International Banking: Recent Trends and Prospects', paper at Banking Conference, April 1976.

Buist, Marten G. *At Spes Non Fracta: Hope and Co., 1770–1817* (The Hague: Nijhoff, 1974).

Cameron, Rondo, 'The Crédit Mobilier and the Economic Development of Europe', *Journal of Political Economy,* 61 (1953) 461–88.

Collis, Maurice, *Wayfoong: The Hong Kong and Shanghai Banking Corporation* (London: Faber, 1965).

Corti, Egon Caesar, *The Reign of the House of Rothschild* (New York: Cosmopolitan Book Corporation, 1928).

Cummings, Richard 'International Credits: Milestones or Millstones', *Journal of Commercial Bank Lending,* (January 1975).

Davis, Steven I. *The Euro-Bank: its Origins, Management and Outlook* (London: Macmillan, 1976).

——, 'How Risky is International Lending', *Harvard Business Review,* 55 (1977) 135–43.

de Roover, Raymond, *The Rise and Decline of the Medici Bank, 1397–1494* (Cambridge, Mass: Harvard University Press, 1963).

Donaldson, T. H. *International Lending by Commercial Banks* (London: Macmillan, 1979).

Ehrenberg, Richard, *Capital and Finance in the Age of the Renaissance* (London: Cape, 1928).

Einzig, Paul *Roll-over Credits: the System of Adaptable Interest Rates* (London: Macmillan, 1973).

Farley, T. M. *The 'Edge Act' and United States International Banking and Finance,* 1962.

Federal Reserve Board, *Federal Reserve Bulletins* – various press releases and surveys.

Feis, Herbert, *Europe, the World's Banker: 1870–1914* (New Haven: Yale University Press, 1930).

Henry, J. A. *The First Hundred Years of the Standard Bank* (London: Oxford University Press, 1963).

Hidy, Ralph, W. *The House of Baring in American Trade and Finance* (Cambridge, Mass: Harvard University Press, 1949).

International Bank for Reconstruction and Development, *Borrowing in International Capital Markets,* E.C. 181/752.

——, *Multilateral Debt Renegotiations, 1956–1968,* E.C. 170.

Jenks, Leland H. *Migration of British Capital to 1875* (New York: Knopf, 1927).

Joslin, David, *A Century of Banking in Latin America* (London: Oxford University Press, 1963).

Kaeuper, Richard, *Bankers to the Crown: the Riccardi of Lucca in the Service of Edward I* (Princeton: Princeton University Press, 1973).

Landes, David S. *Bankers and Pashas: International Finance and Economic Imperialism in Egypt* (London, Heinemann, 1958).

Lary, Hal B. *The United States in the World Economy* (US Department of Commerce, 1943).

Lees, Francis A. *International Banking and Finance* (London: Macmillan, 1974).

Llewellyn, David, *Trends in International Banking and Capital Markets,* Data Series.

Mandich, Donald R. *et al* (eds.), *Foreign Exchange Trading Techniques and Controls* (American Bankers Association, 1976).

Mathis, F. John (ed.) *Offshore Lending by US Commercial Banks* (Bankers Association for Foreign Trade/Robert Morris Associates, 1975).

Mitsui Bank, *The Mitsui Bank: a History of the First Hundred Years* (Tokyo: Mitsui Bank, 1976).

Morgan Guaranty Trust Co. *World Financial Markets.*

Phelps, Clyde, *The Foreign Expansion of American Banks* (New York: Ronald Press, 1927).

Quinn, Brian Scott, *The New Euromarkets* (London: Macmillan, 1975).

Reich, Cary, 'America's New Generation of International Bankers', *Institutional Investor,* June 1977, pp. 37–98.

Robert Morris Associates, *Domestic and International Commercial Loan Charge-offs* (Philadelphia: Robert Morris Associates, 1978).

Ruckdeschel, Fred B. 'Risks in Foreign and Domestic Lending Activities of US Banks', *International Finance Discussion Papers,* no. 66, May 1975.

Salomon Brothers, *Bank Stock Weekly* (New York).

Seidenzahl, Fritz, *1870–1970: 100 Jahre Deutsche Bank* (Frankfurt: Deutsche Bank, 1970).

Société Générale de Belgique, *Société Générale de Belgique: 1822–1972* (Brussels: Société Générale, 1972).

Stern, Siegfried, *The United States in International Banking* (New York: Colombia Press, 1951).

Steuber, Ursel, *International Banking: the Foreign Activities of the Banks of Principal Industrial Countries* (Leiden: Sijthoff, 1976).

Terrell, Henry S. 'Some Current Topics in International Banking', paper presented to American Management Association, April 1975.

Tyson, Geoffrey, *100 Years of Banking in Asia and Africa, 1863–1963 (A*

History of National and Grindlay's Bank Limited) (London: National and Grindlays, 1963).
von Clemm, Michael, 'The Rise of Consortium Banking', *Harvard Business Review* 49 (1971) 125–42.

Index